Library of
Davidson College

Ethnic Politics in Urban America

THE POLISH EXPERIENCE

IN FOUR CITIES

Edited by Angela T. Pienkos

Copyright © 1978 by the Polish American Historical Association
Printed in the United States of America

All rights reserved. No part of this book may be reproduced in any form or by any means without permission in writing from the publisher.

Library of Congress Cataloging in Publication Data

Pienkos, Angela T., editor, Ethnic Politics in Urban America.
Chicago, Illinois: Polish American Historical Association.

7810   780918

ISBN   0-9602162-1-9(paperbound).

For Angela and Joseph Mischke

TABLE OF CONTENTS

Comparing, Contrasting and Generalizing about the Polish American Political Experience: Some Introductory Observations
Angela T. Pienkos 7

Politics and Buffalo's Polish Americans
Walter A. Borowiec 16

Polish Americans in Detroit Politics
Thaddeus C. Radzialowski
with Donald Binkowski 40

The Polish Americans in Milwaukee Politics
Donald E. Pienkos 66

The Limitations of Ethnic Politics:
Polish Americans in Chicago
Edward R. Kantowicz 92

Name Index 106

APPENDICES 109

Appendix 1. Selected Maps.
    1a. Buffalo: Locations of Polish and Italian Foreign Stock Populations, 1970 Census.
    1b. Detroit: Registered Voters Born in Poland, by Precincts—1938.
    1c. Milwaukee: Registered Voters with Polish Surnames—1924.
    1d. Milwaukee: Polish Ethnic Population by Census Tract, 1931-1954.
    1e. Milwaukee: Polish Foreign Stock Population, 1970 Census.
    1f. Chicago: Polish Foreign Stock Population, 1970 Census.
    1g. Chicago: Sources of Electoral Support for Roman Pucinski's 1977 Mayoral Candidacy.

Appendix 2.
    Selected Characteristics of the Political Systems of the Four Cities.

Appendix 3.
    Selected Statistical Data from the 1900, 1930 and 1970 Federal Census for the Four Cities.

Appendix 4.
    Polish Americans holding Elective Political Office in Milwaukee.

CONTRIBUTORS:

Walter A. Borowiec, Associate Professor, Political Science, State University of New York, Brockport.

Edward R. Kantowicz, Associate Professor, History, Carleton University, Ottawa.

Donald E. Pienkos, Associate Professor, Political Science, University of Wisconsin-Milwaukee.

Thaddeus C. Radzialowski, Associate Professor, History, Southwest State University, Marshall, Minnesota.

Donald Bindowski, Judge, Thirty-Seventh District Court, Michigan

Angela T. Pienkos, Chief Administrator, Divine Savior Holy Angels High School, Milwaukee.

Comparing, Contrasting and Generalizing About the Polish American Political Experience: Some Introductory Observations

The ethnic factor in politics has been until recently a neglected subject of American scholarship. This work is a first effort to study the political experience of one major ethnic group. The essays in this collection describe and analyze Polish American political behavior in four leading American cities, Chicago, Detroit, Buffalo and Milwaukee. Each city developed rapidly during the American industrial revolution and attracted large numbers of European immigrants, including masses of Poles who organized their community affairs in a fairly standard fashion. The dominant institutions of Polonia (the term usually used for the neighborhood settlements and organizations formed by Poles and with which they identified) tended everywhere to be the parishes, the fraternal insurance societies, sports and cultural clubs, veterans' groups and the Polish language periodicals. Everywhere, communal leadership, held at first largely by the Catholic clergy, eventually included businessmen, labor leaders, editors, publishers and seekers after public office.[1]

Focusing upon local urban systems, the contributors to this study draw attention to the variations among these cities which differentiated Polish American communities. They describe diverse patterns in ethnic and racial settlement, the composition of groups, municipal government and political competition. Agreeing with the observation made by Robert Lane, that "the seat of ethnic politics is the local community," they avoid the trap of excessive and, on the evidence so far, fruitless generalizations about Polish American ethnicity on the national level.[2] Also, they ably link urban politics and urban ethnicity in America. While each contributor recognizes the historic independence and continuity of Polish American communities, each emphasizes the political forces and structures, and competing social groups, which affected the Polish Americans in their search for political forms and influence.

The essays are, of course, case studies and as is usual with persons from different disciplines (two are historians, two political

---

[1] For some definitions of Polonia see: Helena Lopata, *The Polish-Americans: Status Competition in an Ethnic Community* (Englewood Cliffs, N.J.: Prentice-Hall, 1976) pp. 4, 42-48, 66-67; Edward Kantowicz, *Polish American Politics in Chicago, 1888-1940* (Chicago: University of Chicago Press, 1975) pp. 8-10; Florian Znaniecki, "The Poles," in H.P. Fairchild, ed., *Immigrant Backgrounds* (London and New York: John Wiley Publishers, 1927), pp. 196-211.

[2] Robert Lane, *Political Life: Why People Get Involved in Politics* (Glencoe, Illinois: The Free Press, 1959), p. 239. Efforts to discuss the Polish Americans on the basis of national opinion surveys are characteristic of the research performed by Andrew Greeley, *Ethnicity in the United States: A Preliminary Reconnaissance* (London and New York: John Wiley and Sons, 1974), pp.122-155. His conclusions about the Polish Americans' political behavior are based upon a nationwide

scientists), each author has his own emphasis. Yet, they have much in common. Each discusses the historical development of "his" city's Polish community in roughly similar fashion, providing a setting for analysis of the status of the Polish Americans in contemporary politics. All are concerned to answer the key question of Polish "success" in local politics. All, with the exception of Borowiec on Buffalo, rely heavily upon the Polish language press which flourished in each of the four cities during the first half of the twentieth century. The Polish press is an essential resource since English language newspapers traditionally paid little attention to Polonia. All make extensive use of interviews with Polish Americans knowledgeable about local politics, and the notes to each essay refer to unpublished and printed materials which greatly enrich our understanding of the social dynamics of each community.

Walter Borowiec's article on Polish American politics in Buffalo is dominated by two themes.[3] The first is the effort of Polish American politicians to win the mayoral office, impressively documented in the tendencies of normally Democratic Polish voters to abandon traditional allegiances whenever Republicans nominated a Polish American against a non-Pole. Second, he attempts to explain the behavior of Buffalo Polish Americans (many of whom he interviewed) in terms of their often stormy relationships with the two major party organizations. In analyzing the reasons for their failure to control either organization, Borowiec also develops an interesting four-fold classification of ethnic politicians: "traditional party loyalists," "mavericks," "respectables," and "reformers." He concludes that most Buffalo ethnic politicians continue to be interested mainly in the traditional rewards of patronage and recognition. However, he also argues that social and economic demands upon Buffalo's political system have risen sharply in number, character and intensity in recent years. In these circumstances, the form and goals of ethnic politics are changing, not disappearing, and Polish Americans may become increasingly successful participants in the local arena.

Thaddeus Radzialowski's study, a product of collaboration with Donald Binkowski, is rich in the details of the historic political experience of Detroit's Polonia and presents an interesting

population sample which included 53 Polish American respondents! See also his earlier study, *Why Can't They Be Like Us: America's White Ethnics* (New York: E. P. Dutton, 1972).

[3]Borowiec's essay is revised from the paper he presented at the annual meeting of the Midwest Slavic Conference, May 8, 1976, in Chicago. The contributions by Radzialowski and Binkowski and by Pienkos are original papers which develop upon themes that they discussed at the same conference meeting. Kantowicz's piece is from his monograph on Chicago Polonia politics, the basis for his comments at the meeting.

discussion of the evolution of the meaning of Polish ethnicity over time. Paralleling Borowiec's conclusions on Buffalo, the authors find that Detroit's Poles benefitted from two-party competition for their votes during much of the period between the 1880's and World War I, although they rightly emphasize the religious, class and political bases of the Poles' preference for the Democratic party.[4] Nonetheless, Polish Americans failed to become the dominant force in Detroit politics for several important reasons, among them the existence of the heavily Polish city of Hamtramck, a separate political enclave in the heart of the city's Polonia. Hamtramck's existence siphoned off thousands of votes that otherwise would have been cast for Polish American candidates in Detroit, although the fact that Poles were in political command of a genuine "Polish" city did give Detroiters some sense of pride. Equally significant was the decision in 1918 to "reform" Detroit municipal politics by abolishing aldermanic area wards and establishing instead a system of nonpartisan "at large" elections for city offices. This act effectively neutralized the growing Polish American Democratic electorate. Yet a third major factor in Detroit was the social and economic conflict between the powers-that-be in Detroit industry and the strongly pro-union and heavily Polish working class population of the city. To Radzialowski and Binkowski, this social class conflict lies at the heart of any understanding of Polish American politics in Detroit.

The Milwaukee study by Donald Pienkos resembles the others in a number of respects, but emphasizes three distinguishing features. The first is the constraining effect of the German American majority in the city, a factor that decisively limited the political horizons of the Poles. In a German dominated Milwaukee, the Poles could at best aspire to second in local politics. In no other city in this study was the Polish community so hampered by the dominance of another ethnic group which boasted superiority in population, socio-economic status, cultural influence and organizational strength.

Secondly, intense factionalism inside the Milwaukee Polonia seems to have characterized its history. One wonders why such disturbances were so significant. Perhaps, as the author suggests, incendiary forces in Polonia heightened the conflicts; the presence of the Kruszka brothers, for example, or the popular but anti-establishment Polish socialists. There may be another explanation.

---

[4]The best published work on the subject of the origins and bases of Polish support for the Democratic party prior to 1900 is by Paul Kleppner, *The Cross of Culture* (New York: The Free Press, 1970), pp. 22-67.

Since the Polish American population of Milwaukee was relatively small in comparison to the three other cities, the perceived weakness of the Polish community *vis-a-vis* the Germans may have made it especially conscious of the need to stress solidarity in defense of its interests. Given such a frame of mind, internal political disputes were exaggerated since they were more likely to be seen as vital threats to the entire Polonia.

Thirdly, Pienkos attempts his own characterization of Polish American leadership in Milwaukee politics, one that identifies three succeeding "generational" models, each possessing its own style. His review of the formal rules governing Milwaukee politics (particularly those that reduced the significance of party organization) combined with findings pointing to the gradual assimilation of the Polish American population lead him to be pessimistic about the future possibilities of Polish ethnicity in the community.

Edward Kantowicz's contribution is excerpted from his monograph, *Polish American Politics in Chicago, 1888-1940*, published by the University of Chicago Press in 1975. Some editorial additions bring the analysis up to 1978. Kantowicz attempts to explain why the Chicago Polish Americans failed to elect one of their number as mayor. In his view, this happened because no Polish American politician in Chicago has been able to combine in his own person all the qualities of leadership required to win so high an office in a city characterized by sharp ethnic competitiveness. More importantly, he believes that the

whole thrust of ethnic politics as pursued by the Polish Americans was probably misguided. Ethnic politics, when it means closing ranks in group solidarity and seeking power as a distinct, separate group, has severe limitations. The Polish Americans' large numbers were a disadvantage in two ways: they nurtured the illusion that if Polish voters would only stick together they could gain power and importance by sheer weight of numbers; second, they made other new groups consider the Polish community a threat.

This conclusion seems to be contradicted in part in Buffalo, where politics has been practiced traditionally in a fashion much like Chicago. And, certain developments since the time covered by Kantowicz also lead to some doubt about his assessment. Since 1940, several Polish Americans have mounted serious campaigns to win the office of Chicago mayor, although none has succeeded.

The central issue in each essay is the political success enjoyed by Polish Americans. Though the same question is confronted by all, each proposes different criteria for measuring and evaluating success. This very matter thus deserves some consideration here.

An obvious approach to this question is simply to define political success as the ability to elect Polish American politicans to the office of mayor. By this measure, the Buffalo Polish Americans have been most successful, since they have had three Polish mayors since 1949. Detroit also has had a Polish American as mayor, although he held the post for only one term (1969-73) and did not seek reelection. Furthermore, given Detroit's changing ethnic and racial composition in recent years, it seems unlikely that a second Polish American will emerge as a serious candidate for the office. In Chicago and Milwaukee, Polish Americans have experienced only failure in this respect, although since 1955 three Chicago Poles have tried on four occasions to be elected. In 1955, Benjamin Adamowski ran a strong third in the race for the Democratic party's nomination behind party leader Richard Daley (who was subsequently elected to the first of six four-year terms) and the then incumbent mayor, Martin Kennelly. In 1963, Adamowski ran strong again, this time as the endorsed nominee of the city's weak Republican party. Another Polish Republican, John Waner, attempted to unseat Daley in 1967, only to be overwhelmed. Most recently, Roman Pucinski contested the Democratic primary to fill the position left vacant in December, 1976, when Daley died. Though he received a sizeable proportion of the vote, he was defeated by the organization's nominee, Michael Bilandic, a long-time Daley protege. Furthermore, yet another Polish American political leader, US Congressman Daniel Rostenkowski, has emerged as a serious possible contender for Bilandic's post when his term expires in 1979. In contrast, only one Pole has ever run for mayor in Milwaukee, and his campaign proved to be a dismal failure.

A second measure of success, one discussed less systematically, is the share of a city's elective offices in the possession of Polish Americans. Pienkos argues that Milwaukee Polish Americans achieved significantly in this area over a lengthy span of time, and his data show that Polish Americans held office in roughly the same proportion as their percentage of the total population. Borowiec makes a more impressionistic case for the Buffalo Polish Americans gaining "their share" of the offices. On the other hand, the authors of the Detroit study come to the opposite conclusion. Since 1918, and due to the election reforms instituted in the city, Polish Americans have failed totally in efforts to win their share of the elected offices. They note, however, that Poles have done much better at the county, state and congressional levels and that they have exercised political control over Hamtramck for most of the past fifty years. Kantowicz makes no mention of this criterion of political success; but his analysis of the nature of Chicago machine politics (including the enormous slate-making powers in the hands of Cook County's Democratic party leadership) implies that any measuring of success in terms of the number of elective offices held by itself is probably beside the point.

A third standard of political success, one that is more sophisticated in nature, involves Polish American control over the political party machinery in the cities in which they reside. To what degree have Polish politicians been able to wield such power in their communities? The answer to this question is fairly simple: nowhere have they gained such positions. In the two cities where strong party organizations have existed, Chicago and Buffalo, Poles have never been able to play a decisive role in either the Democratic or the Republican apparatus. Indeed, in both cities, Poles resorted to organizing maverick political movements simply to compel the Irish-dominated Democratic machines to grant them some recognition. In Detroit and Milwaukee, party organizations have played a far less important role in local politics, since local elections are nonpartisan and the vast majority of the electorate is inclined in both cities to vote for the Democrats. Hence, this criterion has little application there, although both Pienkos and Radzialowski point out that Poles have had little success in winning recognition from the organizations that do dominate the nonpartisan nominations and elections—labor unions, good government organizations, and citizens' lobbies.

How can one explain these failures in local politics? Aside from noting constraints growing out of the nature of the political system or from competing ethnic groups in each city, can a more general set of answers be proposed? Two possibilities come to mind. One, advanced by both Borowiec and Kantowicz, concentrates upon the deficiencies in the "Polish national character," primarily the supposed inability of Poles to cooperate in advancing political goals. A second explanation, prominently featured in Radzialowski and Binkowski's work, interprets the political limitations of the Polish Americans in terms of the prejudice they encountered in Detroit. Though suggestive, neither explanation seems to take us very far in answering the main issue of this study. While there is much evidence that seems to back up assertions about the Poles' inability to work together and seeming preference for infighting, one is still left with the nagging question of what actually determines a people's "national character"? And, is national character something that is innate, or best defined in terms of a people's collective historical experience? For the Poles, the history of the past two centuries is one largely associated with political, cultural and economic deprivation. The Poles even lacked their own national state between 1795 and 1918 and thus for five generations had no opportunity to determine their own political destiny. In the United States, the great majority of Polish immigrants were poor, barely literate, and, initially, at least, unfamiliar with the norms and processes of American politics. Given such factors, plus the heritage of political passivity brought to America by the largely peasant immigration, it is difficult to understand how the Poles in America could be expected to compete readily with members of other ethnic groups in the political arena on an equal footing.[5] And, just how far does the prejudice argument bring us? According to the American sociologist Philip Hauser, the Poles' fate, while undeniable, was hardly unique. Reviewing the Chicago experience he writes:

Newcomers in general found their areas of first settlement in the inner, older, least desirable places to live. They did the dirty work with the lowest pay—the work nobody else wanted. In respect to status, newcomer white ethnic groups were treated by those who had come earlier with suspicion, prejudice and even hostility. Nineteenth century immigrants were known as "Krautheads," "Micks," and "dumb Swedes;" eastern and southern European newcomers in the early twentieth century were known as "Wops," "Polacks," "Bohunks," "Sheenies," and the like. There were no exceptions to this rule. In time, as the visibility or audibility of the newcomers disappeared in the second or third generation, the uncomplimentary stereotypes which accompanied them tended to atrophy. This fact, accompanied by improved residential location and higher occupational level and income, was reflected in increased social status and acceptance.[6]

A final explanation for the Polish Americans' political fate can be noted. To what extent have the Polish Americans lacked the necessary political resources to be seriously considered as a factor in the local arena? From our inspection of their fate in four American cities, it might be concluded that up to the present at least, Polish politicians have simply not been strong enough to win entry into their city's "power elite." As early as the nineteenth century, to be

---

[5]For some discussion of elements of the Polish national character, see Lopata, pp. 18-19, 74, 114-115. Greeley emphasizes the historic conditions both in Poland and in America which have shaped the attitudes and behavior of Polish Americans. Greeley, pp. 104, 237-239. See also Lane, pp. 244-245; and Donald Pienkos, "Research on Ethnic Political Behavior Among Polish-Americans: A Review of the Literature," *The Polish Review*, 21 (1976), 135-137.

[6]Philip Hauser, "Chicago—Urban Crisis Exemplar," *Urbanism Past and Present*, 1 (1975-76), 18-19.

sure, Polish immigrants had the vote and because of their large numbers, could influence closely fought elections. Still, prior to the First World War (which culminated in the restoration of an independent Poland, an issue which for many Poles captured the center of the stage), Polish Americans were unable to play a major role in local politics. This was so because Polonia's members were preoccupied with the tasks of simply surviving in their new homeland, busily involved with establishing themselves economically in America, and continuing all the while to assist financially family members left behind in Europe. Also, the early Polish American community lacked the political leadership it needed to gain recognition on an equal basis with representatives of competing ethnic and community groups with which it came into contact in each city. Later on, Polish Americans and their offspring did attain higher economic and occupational status, a development reflected by the increasingly prominent role played by political leaders in Polonia who were better able to articulate ethnic concerns in local affairs. But, at the very time that Polish Americans were reaching higher on the political ladder, the old Polonia communities themselves were beginning to break up, their members becoming acculturated to life and values outside the old neighborhoods. "Americanization"—whether described in generational terms, in the light of growing evidence of intermarriage with non-Poles, in terms of name changes, loss of mastery of the Polish language or resettlement in the suburbs—deprived Polish American politicians of the electoral base they needed to attain political recognition. Again, Polish Americans found themselves lacking a vital resource in their struggle for political success.

Nonetheless, it might be premature to conclude that there is anything irreversible or permanent about this situation. Third and fourth generation Americans of Polish ancestry who are conscious of their ethnicity remain conspicuously active in the politics of each city. Their ability to win elective office may rekindle the sense of ethnic solidarity on the mass level within an increasingly affluent and better educated Polish American population.

In closing, I believe it is most appropriate here to express my thanks to a number of persons and organizations whose great assistance has been instrumental in making this publication possible. First, I would like to acknowledge the University of Chicago for permission to reprint a section of Edward Kantowicz's book on the politics of the Chicago Polonia. All of us connected with this volume particularly appreciate the excellent and original maps drawn by Mr. Donald Temple of the Cartographic Services Laboratory of the University of Wisconsin-Milwaukee. Finally, I wish to express our deep appreciation to the officers and board of directors of the Polish American Historical Association for sponsoring this entire project. Two members of the Association deserve to be singled out for special praise since it was largely through their efforts that this study was realized. Reverend M. J. Madaj, executive secretary of the PAHA, has proven himself a continuing friend of the project at every meeting of the board of directors in which the subject was discussed. Professor Frank Renkiewicz, a past president of the Association and editor of its journal, *Polish American Studies*, offered numerous and useful suggestions for revision of this study.

ANGELA T. PIENKOS
November, 1978

WALTER A. BOROWIEC

Politics and Buffalo's Polish Americans*

Academic interest in ethnicity as a crucial variable in American urban politics continues to grow.[1] Nevertheless, the political behavior of relatively smaller groups like the Poles has not been as thoroughly examined as that of the more numerous Irish, Italians and Jews; and many cities where ethnicity remains important have not been as well researched as, for example, New Haven, Chicago and New York.[2] Consequently, the data for generalizing about ethnic politics are often limited, and the qualitative differences between cities are frequently obscured. The goals of this essay are to describe and to interpret the political behavior of a neglected group, Polish Americans, in a neglected city, Buffalo, using a variety of sources—census tracts, official vote canvasses, local histories, masters' theses and interviews with 83 local Polish political leaders and activists.[3]

Demography

Germans and Irish constituted the largest ethnic groups in Buffalo until the 1890's. Poles began to arrive in significant numbers

---

*The preparation and research for this paper were assisted by a National Endowment for the Humanities Fellowship for College Teachers in Residence in 1975-1976. I should like also to acknowledge the helpful analysis of Donald Rosenthal and Robert Stern, the indispensable assistance of Daniel Kij and Stanley Fronczyk in gaining access to political leaders, and the aid of Maria Walczak, Susan Pajari and my wife Patricia.

[1] In this work, "ethnic" and "ethnicity" refer to the nationality background of recent European immigrants and their American born descendants. Ethnic characteristics in this sense are analytically distinct from racial characteristics. For a discussion of the meanings of "ethnic" see Brett W. Hawkins and Robert A. Lorinskas, eds., *The Ethnic Factor in American Politics* (Columbus, Ohio: Merrill, 1970), Introduction. See also Daniel Patrick Moynihan and Nathan Glazer, *Ethnicity: Theory and Experience* (Cambridge: Harvard University Press), Chapter 1.

[2] Representative of the more recent empirically based studies of ethnic voting are: Raymond Wolfinger, "The Development and Persistence of Ethnic Voting," *American Political Science Review*, 59 (1965), 899-908; Robert A. Lorinskas, Brett W. Hawkins and Stephen Edwards, "The Persistence of Ethnic Voting in Urban and Rural Areas: Results from the Controlled Election Method," *Social Science Quarterly*, 49 (1969), 891-899; Abraham Miller, "Ethnicity and Political Behavior: A Review of Theories and an Attempt at Reformulation," *Western Political Quarterly*, 24 (1971), 483-500; Richard Gabriel, "A New Theory of Ethnic Voting," *Polity*, 4 (1972), 406-38.

[3] The 6th, 9th and 10th wards of Buffalo have been heavily Polish since 1920. After 1972, the old ward system was changed. The Polish wards now correspond to the Polish councilmanic districts, i.e., Fillmore and Lovejoy. Most of the aggregate data in this essay are drawn from these areas. The logical problems in inferring individual voter motivation and attitudes from aggregate data (the ecological fallacy) are clear. Hence, all generalizations should be understood as referring to group trends and characteristics. For a fuller discussion of the survey of Polish leaders see Walter Borowiec, "Perceptions of Ethnic Voters by Ethnic Politicians," *Ethnicity*, 1 (1974), 269-70.

only after 1874, when the first Polish parish, St. Stanislaus', was founded on the East Side. Their original community of about 500 persons grew rapidly through immigration in the next half century, numbering 20,000 by 1890 and between 65,000 and 75,000 (counting both foreign and American born) in 1904.[4] At least as early as 1902, Poles were the most populous ethnic group in the city, followed by Italians, Germans and Irish. The end of liberal immigration policies in the early 1920's curtailed the community's growth. However, in 1970, the growth of the black population since mid-century notwithstanding, Polish Americans (defined as all persons of Polish ethnic ancestry) made up at least one-quarter of the city's 462,000 inhabitants. Their portion of Buffalo's Erie County is even greater. Perhaps as much as 35% to 40% of the combined city and county population is Polish in origin, a basic factor in the electoral success of Polish political candidates.[5]

Until two or three decades ago, the overwhelming majority of Polish Americans in Buffalo lived on the city's East Side. Though the community expanded somewhat to the north and south of its focal parish (at Fillmore and Peckham Streets), the main thrust was eastward. A small subcommunity on the Northwest Side never approached the East Side Polonia in size. The evidence suggests that the East Side is still ethnically homogeneous.[6] Residential patterns, however, have changed somewhat since 1950. The growth of the black community wholly transformed the major Polish neighborhood on its western end. Even before racially related dispersion occurred, many second and third generation Polish Americans sought better housing in the more middle class neighborhoods to the north and northeast. These areas, previously German, are now ethnically heterogeneous.[7] Still more joined the postwar search for the "good life" in suburbia, and many of the city's suburbs, particularly to the east, have large numbers of Polish Americans. Cheektowaga, for example, a "town" of over 100,000 on

---

[4]Rosemary Switala, "The Political Growth and Development of the Polish Community in Buffalo," M. A. Thesis, State University of New York at Buffalo, 1963, p. 12; Niles Carpenter and Daniel Katz, "Acculturation of the Polish Group in Buffalo," *University of Buffalo Studies* (1929), 103.

[5]Many of the leaders interviewed suggested a much higher figure, 45% to 50%, an estimate that should be approached skeptically. There is a need for a more accurate census. For a brief, somewhat polemical discussion of the issue of statistical assimilation by the Census Bureau see "Discrimination in the Census Bureau," *EMPAC* (Newsletter), July, 1976, 12.

[6]The 1960 Census tracts for Buffalo indicate that, next to the blacks, the Poles were the "most segregated" group in the city, that is, they tended to be highly concentrated in specific geographic areas. Of the 47,600 of Polish foreign stock, 61% lived in census tracts of heavy Polish (i.e., more than 50% Polish foreign stock) concentration. I am indebted to Dr. Robert H. Stern of the Political Science Department, State University of New York at Buffalo, for his unpublished material analyzing ethnic concentration in Buffalo.

[7]The existence of an identifiable contemporary German American cultural community is doubtful. Though the old German neighborhoods have disappeared, some Polish leaders believe there is a lingering German identification and ethnic vote among many Buffalo residents.

Buffalo's eastern boundary is predominantly Polish.

Buffalo's Polonia closely follows the classic immigrant pattern of gradual upward social mobility. Initially, it was largely working class in occupation and education. Census data for selected tracts in the core settlement area indicate that these are still predominantly working class.[8] By the 1920's, however, an ethnic lower middle class—shopkeepers, tavern owners and small entrepreneurs—had appeared on the East Side. Today, the community also has a sizeable upper-middle class of professionals and successful businessmen which tends to reside in ethnically mixed neighborhoods or suburbs. It provides many of the "respectables" for public office as well as organizational and community leaders.

Polish Americans in Buffalo are overwhelmingly Roman Catholic, though there is an important Polish National Catholic parish in the original settlement, a product in part of early Polish-Irish conflict in the hierarchy of the diocese. Here as elsewhere in Polonia, the associational life of the neighborhood focused upon the parish, and the influence of the pastor was enormous in the immigrant period.[9] Father John Pitass particularly, the founder of the first Polish American parish, was a powerful spiritual and temporal leader, still remembered by older individuals with awe, respect and trembling.[10] By contrast, the contemporary clergy lack the pervasive social and political influence of the old pastors, and the church does not dominate the lives of parishioners as it once did. Political leaders seem agreed that the Polish clergy is not now an overtly significant factor in local politics.

Besides the church, an extensive network of voluntary associations attracted a large and active membership. At one time, Buffalo's Polonia had over one hundred dramatic societies, fraternal groups, singing societies, youth groups and gymnastic clubs. It also had its own Polish language daily newspaper, *Dziennik dla Wszystkich* (Everybody's Daily News). However, this rich ethnic social structure has diminished considerably since the 1950's. *Dziennik* has ceased publication, and membership in all but

---

[8]The proportion of "operatives" in Polish census tracts in 1960 was 34.9% (25.6% in the city as a whole), "professional" and "managerial" about 4% (8% in the city), and "sales,-- 3.6% (6.1% in the city).

[9]Edward Kantowicz, *Polish American Politics in Chicago* (Chicago: University of Chicago Press, 1975), pp. 30-33; Donald Pienkos, "Politics, Religion and Change in Polish Milwaukee," *Wisconsin Magazine of History*, 61 (1978), 179-209; Thaddeus Radzialowski, "The View from the Polish Ghetto," *Ethnicity*, 1 (1974), 125-150.

[10]Several older leaders commented on Pitass' willingness to advise his flock on the "right" candidates. There is some evidence that Pitass cooperated with some city officials on land acquisition for his parishioners. See Walter Borowiec, "The Prototypical Ethnic Politician: A Study of the Political Leadership of an Ethnic Subcommunity," Diss., State University of New York at Buffalo, 1972, pp. 63-65.

a few voluntary associations has declined. Many organizations have disappeared entirely. Polish leaders believe that the few which remain are not important political interest groups.[11] There are clear signs that today's Polish population is quite different from the immigrant community of the past.[12] Moreover, it has been dispersed to a degree in recent years, becoming more middle class, suburban and acculturated.[13] One is tempted, therefore, to conclude that the political salience of Polish ethnicity has faded, if not disappeared. As we shall see, this is not the case.

Voting Patterns

The behavior of voters in the Polish wards reveals two, at times, conflicting trends. First, since 1928, the Polish vote has been strongly Democratic. Secondly, it has been a cohesive ethnic bloc when the opportunity has existed in local politics.[14] This was not, however, always so. The earliest successes of Polish Americans took place in the 1890's. Jacob Rozan was the first of their number to win elective office as county supervisor in 1891, and the following year, Jacob Johnson (Jasiek) was the first Pole to hold office as alderman.[15] Both were Democrats. Francis Horski was elected in 1895 as an at-large member of the city council on the Republican ticket. In this early period, Polish Americans in Buffalo did not align themselves wholly with either major party. Both Democratic and Republican Poles were elected regularly and party registrations were fairly evenly divided. Intense inter-party competition divided the East Side with neither side able to claim the Polish vote.

The list of Polish successes and "firsts" grew rapidly in the two decades after 1890. The Poles did suffer two setbacks, however, both related to the structural-institutional characteristics of the local political system. A gerrymander in 1906 redrew ward boundaries to create a single, very populous Polish district and split

[11] Many leaders noted an indirect political function of the few remaining voluntary associations. They provide a network of contacts which politicans may use to seek popularity, and they serve as a communications link between voters and leaders. Since 1960, a weekly English language paper, the *AM-Pol Eagle* has provided news about Polonia. Detroit and Chicago have a variety of daily and weekly publications in both languages. Wisconsin's only remaining Polish newspaper is the weekly *Gwiazda Polarna*, published in Stevens Point.

[12] Eugene Obidinski, "From Ethnic Group to Status Group: A Study of the Polish American Subcommunity in Buffalo," Diss., State University of New York at Buffalo, 1968, pp. 57-59.

[13] The terms "acculturated" and "assimilated" need to be distinguished from one another. For a discussion of the diverse process that this distinction implies see Michael Parenti, "Ethnic Politics and the Persistence of Ethnic Identification," *American Political Science Review*, 61 (1967), 716-18.

[14] There is considerable disagreement and confusion about what constitutes an ethnic vote and how it is measured. For an excellent discussion of the problem see Martin Plax, "Uncovering Ambiguities in Some Uses of the Concept of Ethnic Voting," *Midwest Journal of Political Science*, 15 (1971), 571-82. An interesting attempt to disentangle the effects of candidate ethnicity and sense of party identification is provided by Robert A. Lorinskas, *et al*, "The Persistence of Ethnic Voting..." It might help to define an ethnic vote as clearly present when the following conditions hold: 1. a non-group member opposes a co-ethnic candidate; 2. the non-group candidate is a member of the party which that particular group traditionally supports (i.e., the co-ethnic belongs to the opposing party); 3. a large majority of voters support their co-ethnic (i.e., traditional party ties are ignored).

[15] Switala, pp. 18-20.

off fringes of the community, submerging them in neighboring Irish and German wards.[16] Consequently, the number of Polish county supervisors who were elected by ward declined from three to one. Then, in 1916, the city charter was revised to establish a commission form of government. One provision provided for the at-large election of city commissioners with both legislative and administrative powers. The elimination of areal aldermanic districts and the imposition of at-large elections had at least one significant effect: not one Pole was elected to city government from 1916 to 1927.[17]

Two events in the late 1920's altered the situation. A new city charter in 1927 rearranged ward boundaries and re-established areal councilmanic seats. By 1930, two seats were again in Polish hands and have remained there to this day. The restructuring of city government assured Polonia of a minimal degree of representation and gave community leaders important bases for reaching higher office. The presidential candidacy of Al Smith in 1928 also made a considerable difference. The son of immigrants and possessing a strongly ethnic political style and appeal, a Catholic, a "wet" and a New Yorker as well, Smith won an extraordinarily large Polish vote (Table 1). As Samuel Lubell has pointed out, the Smith candidacy inaugurated a major shift in ethnic partisan loyalties and voting behavior.[18] The Depression and Franklin Roosevelt's presidency accelerated the shift to the Democratic party until, by the end of the 1930's, real party competition, when the ethnic factor was held constant, had nearly ceased to exist on the East Side.

The Democratic loyalties of Polish Americans are clear in several ways. Table 2 shows the change in their party registrations. They have not voted for a Republican presidential candidate since Coolidge (Table 1) and Democratic candidates for state offices— governor, senator, supreme court judge, attorney general—can expect heavy majorities from the East Side of Buffalo. In local elections, particularly those for areal seats, Democrats dominate when both parties run Polish candidates and neutralize the ethnic factor. Out of 117 local areal elections in which both parties nominated Polish Americans from 1928 to 1972, the Democrats won 100 times.

---

[16]*Ibid.*
[17]On the possible historical correlations between ethnicity and a shift to the mayor-council system in several other cities see Daniel N. Gordon, "Immigrants and Urban Governmental Forms in American Cities, 1933-1960," *American Journal of Sociology*, 73 (1968), 158-71.
[18]Samuel Lubell, *The Future of American Politics* (New York: Doubleday Anchor Books, 1956), pp. 29-41.

Table 1
Percentage of the Two Party Vote for President
in Polish American Wards — 1920-1976

Year	% Democrat	% Republican
1920	49.6	50.4
1924	44.9	49.0
1928	72.0	28.0
1932	71.6	28.4
1936	79.3	20.7
1940	82.4	17.6
1944	80.6	19.4
1948	80.0	20.0
1952	67.3	32.7
1956	54.0	46.0
1960	75.1	24.9
1964	84.4	15.6
1968+	73.4	17.4
1972	55.8	44.2
1976	65.5	34.5

+A Polish American, Edmund Muskie, was the Democratic vice presidential nominee in 1968; George Wallace's third party candidacy attracted 9.2 per cent of the Polish American vote.
Source: *Official Canvasses of the Vote for Erie County* on file at the Erie County Board of Elections.

Table 2
Major Party Enrollment in Three Polish Wards and Entire City
Selected Years 1920-1970

Year	6th Ward Dem.	6th Ward Rep.	9th Ward Dem.	9th Ward Rep.	10th Ward Dem.	10th Ward Rep.	Total City Dem.	Total City Rep.	Percentage of Total City Enrollment Represented by Three Polish Wards
1920	—	—	47.8	46.5	61.2	34.7	32.4	61.2	3.5
1928*	60.0	38.5	42.9	51.8	40.0	58.0	33.2	65.0	10.5
1940	70.3	23.2	60.8	37.5	60.3	37.8	50.5	42.4	9.5
1949	75.5	22.6	66.5	31.5	66.0	32.1	47.5	49.0	11.7
1960-61	73.4	25.2	66.5	31.4	64.4	33.8	55.4	41.5	10.3
1969-70	71.7	25.6	70.7	26.4	68.8	28.2	61.3	34.4	9.7
1975-76# Fillmore			74.2 Dem. 22.2 Rep.				66.5	28.2	22.7
1975-76 Lovejoy			69.3 Dem. 26.3 Rep.						

*6th ward not considered Polish until after 1929. Prior to that time parts of the 6th were included in the 10th and in non-Polish wards.

#Beginning in 1972, ward apportionment was altered—"Polish wards" now denoted by names of councilmanic districts, Lovejoy and Fillmore.

Sources: Switala, p.35; official enrollment figures on file at Erie County Board of Elections.

Yet, at the same time Polish voters have coalesced behind Polish Republicans who were slated against non-Polish Democrats. In some cases the deviation of the normally Democratic Polish wards has been remarkable, and one quantitative study of the relative cohesiveness of ethnic groups in Buffalo has concluded that the Poles rank first in supporting "their own."[19] The mayoral race of 1949 illustrates this behavior best. In the spring of 1949, Buffalo Polonia appeared to be in the enviable position of choosing between two Slavic Americans. The Democrats had endorsed County Clerk Steve Pankow, a Ukrainian American closely identified with Buffalo's Polish community, and the Republicans had nominated City Councilman Joseph Mruk. Then, a divisive Democratic primary eliminated Pankow in favor of an Irish American, City Judge John Hillary. Charges that Hillary was anti-Polish together with the historic opportunity presented by the Mruk candidacy gave the GOP a landslide in the normally Democratic Polish wards and helped elect Buffalo's first Polish American mayor (Table 3).

Table 3
Vote for Mayor, Polish American Wards, 1937-1977

Year	Democratic	Republican	Significant Third Party
1937	50.0	21.2	28.8
1941	70.5	29.5	—
1945	69.3	30.7	—
1949#	14.0	86.0	—
1953	81.4	18.6	—
1957#	25.5	65.6	8.9
1961#X	42.3	51.4	6.3
1965	36.3	63.7	—
1969#	32.3	66.0	1.7
1973X	86.2	13.8	—
1977*	22.0	27.8	50.2

#The Republican candidate in this election was Polish.
XThe Democratic candidate in this election was Polish.

*In 1977, the incumbent Democratic mayor, Stanley Makowski, did not run for re-election. Arthur Eve, a black state legislator who had gained something of a national reputation for his participation in the negotiations surrounding the Attica prison riot, captured the Democratic party nomination in the primary election. In the general election, the Republicans ran an Irish American and a third party, the Conservatives, ran another Irish American, James Griffin. Griffin was able to capitalize on what many observers described as a back-lash vote against Eve and was elected.

[19]Dale Bodnar, "Ethnic Bloc Voting in Buffalo," Senior Honors Thesis, State University of New York at Buffalo, 1968, pp. 57-60.

There are other examples of Poles switching from their normal Democratic allegiance when the Republicans nominated a Pole against a non-Pole (Table 3). In 1957, Chester Kowal, another Polish Republican, rolled up large majorities on the East Side. He lost the election by 60 votes only because a third party candidate split the Republican coalition. Kowal carried the Polish wards and was elected in 1961, though this election was unusual since both major party candidates were Polish and another, a third party candidate (the incumbent Democratic Mayor Frank Sedita) complicated the contest. As recently as 1969, a Republican Polish mayoral candidate, Alfreda Slominski, carried two-thirds of the East Side vote against a non-Pole. Just one year earlier the Democratic presidential candidate, Hubert Humphrey, had carried the area overwhelmingly. Similar ticket-splitting on behalf of Republican ethnics is evident at other times as well.

Table 3 not only indicates ticket splitting among Buffalo's Poles; it hints at the extraordinary success they have had in winning the mayoralty since 1949. In the eight elections from 1949 to 1977, a Pole ran in all but three (1953, 1965, 1977). In 1961, both Democrats and Republicans nominated Polish Americans. Three of the eight races ended in Polish victories, and in one other the Republican Kowal lost by the narrowest margin in Buffalo's history. Buffalo has had three Polish mayors—Mruk, Kowal and Stanley Makowski—while Polish communities in Chicago and Milwaukee have yet to elect their first. Undoubtedly, the cohesive ethnic character of the Polish vote and these electoral successes are related. Ethnicity still has an impact at the ballot box, much to the advantage of several Polish politicians in Buffalo.

Party Politics: Feuding Democrats

Despite electoral success, some Polish leaders remain dissatisfied. In part, these sentiments grow out of their weakness in the local party structure, a factor which, owing to a qualitatively different relationship with the two major parties, operates differently in each one. Though Poles have contributed importantly to Democratic victories and have served on the party's county executive committee, they have never been at the controls. The chairman of the Erie County Democratic party at the apex of the local organization holds significant power over nominations, campaign strategy and funding, patronage and (to a lesser extent) the formulation of positions on public issues. No Pole has held this office, which for the past three decades has been an Irish preserve. Several of the leaders interviewed for this study noted these facts as signs of the weakness of Poles in party affairs. Indeed, until recently many Polish leaders looked upon the party organization as an Irish conspiracy to subvert Polish power, causing numerous intra-party ethnic skirmishes with Polish generals leading the dissidents. If party loyalty is a mark of political skill, then Democrats in Buffalo's Polonia have much to learn from their Irish colleagues.[20] Until lately, the relationship between Polish Democrats and their party is best described by words like factionalism, dissatisfaction, distrust and hostility.

There is a historical basis for Polish paranoia. The "Polish gerrymander" and charter revisions early in the century represented, at least in part, attempts to dilute Polish electoral strength. In the 1920's and 1930's, Poles demanded recognition by way of endorsed nominations to higher offices — congressman mayor, judge of the state supreme court, councilman at-large, countywide positions — to which they had never been nominated. In the mid-1930's, several young Polish activists concluded that the only way to gain sufficient recognition from the major parties was through a third party. Consequently, in 1936 and 1937, they organized the EC-POLE party — EC-POLE being an acronym for Erie County Pole. Though some EC-POLE leaders were Republicans, most were dissident Democrats who had the covert support of the leading Polish Democrat, John Ulinski.[21] The party ran nominees for federal and state offices in 1936 and a full slate, including a mayoral candidate, in 1937. Its campaign in 1936 was buried in the Roosevelt landslide, but in 1937 it produced the desired effect. The Polish vote was split, and Democratic nominees lost their normal 65 to 75% margins, throwing the election to the Republicans. The EC-POLE nominee for mayor, Joseph Kaszubowski, defeated the Republican nominee and held the Democratic vote to 50% in the Polish wards (Table 3). Thereafter, the major parties demonstrated willingness to nominate and elect Poles to higher office. Polish Democrats in particular were quite satisfied with the results of the EC-POLE movement and their dissident tendencies declined for a few years.

[20]On the Irish and party loyalty see Edward Levine, *The Irish and Irish Politicians* (Notre Dame, Ind.: University of Notre Dame Press, 1966), p. 178.
[21]The information on the EC-POLE party is derived mostly from party members who were available for interviews. Many of them are politically still active and have requested anonymity. There is very little on the EC-POLE movement in the English-language press. John Ulinski served in a variety of legislative, administrative and party offices, including a stint as one of President Truman's Boundary Commissioners. "The Great Johnny U," according to older politicians, was the closest to a Polish boss that the Buffalo Polonia ever produced.

Matters returned to their prior chaos in 1949. The candidate of the Polish Democrats, Steve Pankow, was defeated in the spring primary, leaving many older leaders convinced that the Irish bosses really favored their fellow ethnic, Hillary. The primary campaign inaugurated a series of intra-party conflicts lasting until 1965. These feuds involved a variety of elections and patronage matters, but they tended to become especially bitter in the mayoral campaigns. In 1953, for example, the leadership endorsed a German for mayor, and Pankow challenged its decision in the primary with the support of dissidents who wished to retaliate for the Hillary affair. Pankow won both the primary and the regular election. Once in office, he and the venerable John Ulinski forced a change in party leadership. For reasons unknown the Polish faction did not then demand that one of their own be named chairman, and Peter Crotty was elected to the post. If Pankow and Ulinski had hoped to be senior partners in the new Irish-Polish alliance, they were soon disappointed. Crotty quickly established control, effectively using patronage, the growing black vote, Ulinski's death in 1958, and the legal barrier to Pankow succeeding himself. So adept was he that Theodore White ranked him among the last of the old style urban bosses in 1960.[22] Crotty's power assured the Italian American judge, Frank Sedita, of the Democratic mayoral endorsement in 1957. This incensed several Polish Democrats, but since the GOP had nominated a Pole, Chester Kowal, they were content to watch their party go down to defeat in what they thought would be a repetition of 1949. Their strategy failed. A third party candidate, Elmer Lux, split the Republican vote to the disadvantage of Kowal. Meanwhile, Sedita rolled up huge majorities in the Italian and black wards and won the election.

With his candidate in City Hall, Crotty consolidated his influence. The organization secured a charter revision enabling incumbent mayors to seek re-election. This provision, the absence of which had severely hampered Mruk and Pankow, appeared to set the stage for Sedita's continuation in office. Several Polish Democrats concluded that in this case Crotty's power would hinder Polish access to patronage positions and nominations to other offices. Consequently, the campaign of 1961 witnessed another Polish insurrection, now led by Victor Manz, a councilman from the small Polish community on the Northwest side.[23] Although

---

[22] Theodore White, *The Making of the President, 1960* (New York: Atheneum, 1961), pp. 139-40.

[23] The description of the Manz campaign is based heavily on an interview with Manz himself and on the comments of other respondents.

Manz was identifiably Polish, his background, values and political style were more middle class and reform oriented than ethnic. Throughout his political career he had emphasized issues rather than his ethnicity, winning a reputation as a leader who was knowedgeable about such community concerns as air pollution, race relations, crime and education. As an opponent of any strong party chairman, whether Irish or Polish, Manz also had demonstrably middle class attitudes toward the party organization. Crotty's "bossism" became a key issue in the primary. Despite his "respectable" and reform image, Manz did not disavow his ethnic background. He reminded ward leaders and office holders how poorly they had been treated by Crotty, addressed several meetings in Polish, and performed all the symbolic actions that candidates must do in order to win Polish votes in Buffalo.[24]

Manz accomplished what many had thought impossible, defeating an incumbent and endorsed Democratic mayor in the primary.[25] Ethnic appeal, the support of many Polish ward and precinct leaders, and the image of an anti-boss reform candidate were the chief factors in his upset victory. Once nominated, Manz attacted overt support from Polish Democrats who were eager to remove Crotty. The losers refused to accept the results, however, and Sedita ran as an independent. Many non-Polish party leaders and workers supported him rather than Manz in the fall. Meanwhile, the GOP renominated Kowal, thereby fragmenting the Polish vote. Crotty and Sedita, according to some leaders, knew they would lose. Crotty in particular felt it necessary to run Sedita in order to defeat Manz and prevent his replacement as county chairman. The strategy worked. Kowal and Manz split the Polish vote while Sedita carried the Italian wards and many black precincts. Kowal swept the middle class Republican neighborhoods to give him the margin of victory. The failure of the machine to back Manz who, after all, was their official nominee, embittered many Polish Democratic leaders. More than ever they were convinced that the party stood in the way of Polish interests.

[24]Three Polish party leaders (ward chairmen) publicly endorsed Manz. The fact that they were "payrollers" (incumbents of patronage positions) testifies to Manz' support among traditional ethnic leaders. All three were dismissed from office as a result of their endorsement.

[25]Manz won the Democratic primary by 437 votes, accumulating heavy majorities in only nine of Buffalo's twenty-seven wards. Sedita carried the other eighteen. Manz was strongest in the five most heavily Polish wards; in the 6th. 9th, amd 10th wards he overwhelmed Sedita 6,062 to 1,066. Though Sedita swamped Manz in the two heavily Italian wards, 3,328 to 786, he was unable to overcome Manz' lead. Switala, p. 84.

Crotty retired voluntarily in 1964. Since then Chairman Joseph Crangle has mended intra-party ethnic divisions. An adept political broker, Crangle successfully moderated the factionalism of black, Polish, Irish and Italian leaders.[26] Although he engineered Sedita's nomination and election in 1965 and 1969, he recognized Polish Americans in endorsements and patronage. Crangle's skill in organizing campaigns and turning out the vote together with a growing Democratic majority in Erie County gave his party control of the sheriff's, district attorney's and comptroller's offices.[27] These long-time Republican fiefdoms carried significant patronage, which Crangle parceled out with meticulous concern for ethnic recognition. Many formerly fire-breathing Polish mavericks suddenly found themselves "on the payroll." Their willingness to sing the praises of party loyalty increased remarkably. Since 1969, many more party loyalists have appeared in Polonia. In some ways they resemble the machine politicians of Chicago more than their ancestors in Buffalo. Party loyalty, they may have discovered also has rewards other than the public payroll. In 1973, the Democratic party endorsed and elected a Polish mayoral candidate for the first time.[28]

Party Politics: Loyal Republicans

The success of Polish Republicans in Buffalo has been remarkable. Since 1940, two mayors, a state supreme court judge, a congressman, a county clerk, a county judge and a county comptroller have been drawn from their ranks. No more than the Poles among the Democrats, however, have they controlled the party's machinery. Their success can be attributed to a variety of factors: (a) the propensity of Polish Democrats to support Polish Republican candidates; (b) the rational response of the Republican leadership in recognizing this fact and nominating Poles; (c) the unswerving party loyalty of most Polish Republicans. The tendency of Polish Democrats to cross over is clear, but Republican

---

[26] Many older Polish mavericks do not think Crangle is much of an improvement over Crotty in the matter of Polish recognition. However, even they admit that he has some enviable political skills. Moreover, he does not inspire the same depth of hatred as Crotty.

[27] Party registration at the Erie County Board of Elections showed 481,706 registered voters in the county. Of these, 246,242 (51.1%) were Democrats, and 199,374 (41.4%) were Republicans. Of the city's 162,277 registered voters, 107,982 (66.5%) are Democrats, and 45,774 (28.2%) are Republicans.

[28] Makowski's election did not placate some dissident Democrats, though most Poles in the party are loyalists. They contend that Makowski did not respond sufficiently to Polish claims in his patronage appointments. Note, for example, the interview with a noted Buffalo Democrat reprinted in the *Kosciuszko Foundation Newsletter* (1975), pp.4-5.

willingness to run Polish candidates deserves some extended comment. After 1945, the Republicans, led by County Chairman Harry Foreman, adopted a calculated ethnic strategy for the sake of a winning margin in city elections.[29] The Mruk candidacy in 1949 brought gratifying results, and since then the strategy has been repeated often for other offices.

Though Polish Republicans often urged their party to make a stronger appeal in their neighborhoods, they could not demand recognition. Their wards are populated by voters who normally vote Democratic, meaning that the "clout" of Polish Americans in the Republican establishment is minimal. Since they do not represent reliable components of the normal Republican coalition, they may request, cajole and persuade, but they may not demand. When the party leadership deems it wise to slate a particularly attractive Polish candidate, it does so out of rational self-interest rather than to accede to demands for recognition. Moreover, Republicans in Buffalo have never made a *sustained* organizational effort to convert Polish voters from their Democratic habits as they did, for example, among the Italians of New Haven, Connecticut. There, the GOP won the allegiance of a normally Democratic ethnic group for the long term after a grass roots effort of several years. Their successes notwithstanding, Polish leaders in the Erie County GOP have remained spokesmen for a minority within a minority of the party.[30]

Polish Republicans are unusually loyal to their party. With some important exceptions, they tend to be "organization men" far more than their Democratic peers. Of 52 Polish Democratic politicians interviewed for this study, 32 (62%) rated loyalty in party service "very important"; 23 of the 30 Polish Republican leaders (77%) placed the same value on party loyalty. The average Polish Republican must be a loyalist. If he is a ward chairman or party functionary, he may depend entirely on the party for his job. And since the party does not endorse mavericks, the Polish Republican who hopes to be endorsed for an office which is competitive must be loyal. He must tend to ward committee work, attend fund-raisers, campaign for other endorsed candidates and be ready to run as a "sacrificial lamb" in areal contests. This seems to be the only way to attain political success, since the means available to Polish Democrats (such as running as an independent) are foreclosed.

---

[29]Switala, pp. 60-61. Several older leaders confirmed Foreman's receptivity to a Polish candidate for mayor. In 1949, an ethnic strategy was unnecessary in county elections since the GOP held an edge in county registration.
[30]Robert Dahl, *Who Governs?* (New Haven: Yale University Press, 1961).

Republican Poles in elective office are only slightly more advantaged than party leaders holding patronage jobs. They may have a bit more independence and clout in the party, but should they become too independent, the leadership can threaten opposition in the primary. This particularly encourages party discipline because most elected Polish Republican office holders are among the six at-large councilmen rather than the nine areal councilmen. If the party refuses endorsement, it can turn out large majorities in non-Polish neighborhoods where its registration far exceeds that in Polish precincts. Thus, the simple statistics of partisan registration impose major constraints upon Polish Republicans.

There have been exceptions to the rules among Polish Republicans. One of the most notable has been Mrs. Alfreda Slominski. Though a successful candidate on the Republican ticket, she can hardly be called a loyalist. She has never held party office and was required to run un-endorsed in her first attempt to win public office (councilman at-large). Furthermore, Slominski is a frequent critic of her party's leaders but, except for a defeat in the mayoral election of 1969, she has done quite well. She owes her success to an appeal which cuts across the normal ethnic loyalties of Buffalo politics and is associated with problems connected with the changing racial balance in the city. Her career in politics began with an appointment to the city school board. In this office and later, as a member of the city council, she was associated with racially charged issues. Deservedly or not, people considered Slominski "anti-black," for "law and order" and for neighborhood schools. Buffalo liberals tended to dismiss her as a local version of Boston's Louise Day Hicks.

Slominski's critics overlooked certain points. Most obviously, her success indicated the strength of views that both parties had ignored and her style had a decidedly "middle class" character, that is, she emphasized honesty, efficiency and nonpartisanship in her statements and behavior. For example, one of her crusades in the city council was a quixotic attempt (given the 13-2 Democratic edge in the body) to challenge the qualifications of patronage appointments. She even criticized Polish job holders as incompetent or unqualified.[31] The stance of crusader-reformer against corruption has been as important in her appeal as identification with racial issues and has given her widespread popularity among non-Polish voters. Whatever its exact basis,

---

[31]Traditional, older Democrats never forgave her for this transgression. They publicly supported Sedita in 1969, in part because her criticisms had offended many of them and their allies.

Slominski's appeal has won her a measure of political success within the Republican party as a maverick.[32]

Contemporary Polish American Leadership Styles - A Typology

Two variables commonly figure in discussions of ethnic politicians. One, the relationship between ethnic leaders and local party structures, focuses on the question of party loyalty. The other is the difference between ethnic and non-ethnic perceptions of the nature of politics and political rewards.

Party loyalty—a central theme of this study—can be conceived of as a variable involving a wide range of characteristics, behavior and attitudes. It embraces such activities as party support in campaigns and primaries, party committee work, party solidarity and cooperation in patronage and nomination decisions. There is an attitudinal dimension as well, including, for example, the perceptions of the constraints and advantages of party structures among political leaders. Two aspects of party loyalty may be abstracted for purposes of this discussion. A high degree of party loyalty describes the political leader who has held party office prior to holding public office, who supports organizational choices in nominations and appointments, who never runs against an endorsed candidate in a primary, who cooperates with the party on campaign funding and strategy and who perceives party service and loyalty as prerequisite to political success. Conversely, low party loyalty may be ascribed to someone who is critical of his party, runs against an endorsed incumbent or on a third party ticket, finds it unnecessary to belong to the ward organization and assumes generally that political success is possible without organizational loyalty.

The second variable, again at the risk of oversimplification, may be treated in dichotomous fashion. It is based on the work of several authors — Lane, Dahl, Wolfinger, Banfield and Wilson among others — which indicates that qualitative differences exist between ethnic and non-ethnic politics.[33] Though they employ somewhat different concepts in a general way to refer to "contextual" or "systemic" variables, these writers agree on certain

---

[32]Even Mrs. Slominski needed the normal non-Polish vote to win. She lost the 1969 mayoral election by 20,000 votes, approximately the margin by which she lost in the northern Republican wards.

[33]Robert Lane, *Political Life* (New Haven: Yale Press, 1959), p. 240; Dahl, pp. 52-54; Raymond Wolfinger, "Some Consequences of Ethnic Politics," in M. Kent Jennings and Harmon Ziegler, eds., *The Electoral Process* (Englewood Cliffs, N. J.: Prentice-Hall, 1966), pp. 47-49; Edward Banfield and James Q. Wilson, *City Politics* (Cambridge, Mass.: Harvard University Press, 1963), pp. 155, 414.

fundamental matters which serve a discussion of ethnic leadership. They accept of course the high probability that there is a specifically ethnic perception of politics and political rewards. Ethnic politicians interpret politics as a struggle among groups that are racial, ethnic or religious in character rather than based on class interests. The benefits they seek are "recognition" and the tangible, divisible rewards of patronage. Recognition is the symbolic gratification of a group's collective psyche. Those who are recognized (i.e., ethnic leaders who are nominated or appointed) also benefit tangibly. Getting "your people" nominated, elected and "on the payroll"; distributing individual favors and service — these are the main objectives. Ethnic politicians in this view are not particularly interested in collective tangible rewards for their group. Neither the programs nor the policies they implement in office are important, though they may be significant for many of the co-ethnics.[34] Collective benefits, aside from symbolic recognition, are not important to the ethnic leader. Traditional ethnic leaders vie over which group will gain office instead of what will be done with the power of the office.

Another set of perceptions — sometimes known as the "middle class" or "Anglo" ethos, sometimes simply called a non-ethnic world view — stands in sharp contrast to the first.[35] Politics in this case involves debate and conflict over programs and issues; it is not, however, group conflict, but a contest among individuals over policy alternatives. Public interest, not group interest, is supposed to determine political decisions. Since symbolic recognition would constitute a false basis for political debate, the political process should focus on what policy alternatives leaders represent rather than the group they come from. In some variations of this world view the legitimacy of one social aggregate—class—is acceptable provided that politics stresses tangible, not symbolic, rewards.[36] In this view, ethnicity obscures the "real," that is, the class cleavages that pervade the political process. A final element in the non-ethnic perception of politics emphasizes the virtues of honesty, efficiency and non-partisanship, particularly in local politics. Politicians above all must not betray the public trust by seeking gain for themselves and their group through the political

---

[34] See Walter A. Borowiec, "Persistance and Change in the Gatekeeper Role of Ethnic Leaders: The Case of the Polish-American," *Political Anthropology*, 1 (1975).
[35] Banfield and Wilson, pp. 229-49; James Q. Wilson and Edward Banfield, "Public Regardingness as a Value Premise in Voting Behavior," *American Political Science Review*, 58 (1964), 976-77.
[36] Wolfinger emphasizes class politics in opposition to ethnic politics. For a dissenting view see Daniel Patrick Moynihan and Nathan Glazer, *Beyond the Melting Pot* (Cambridge, Mass.: Harvard University Press, 1963), pp. 301-3.

system. Rational, scientific criteria for decision-making should prevail. And since a person's qualifications, not his name or party affiliation, determine appointments, nominations and elections, the basic justification for patronage and recognition must be rejected.

Four combinations of these two dichotomous variables are possible. They are outlined in Figure 1. Each cell in this two-by-two graph represents a pure type of leadership among Polonia politicians. Altogether of of course they refer to ideal categories, but the typology is a useful summary of the complexity of one group's contemporary political leadership.

FIGURE 1

A Typology of Buffalo's Polish American Leadership

Degree of Party Loyalty	Perception of Political System and Political Rewards	
	Ethnic	Non-Ethnic
High	Traditional Loyalists	Respectables
Low	Mavericks	Reformers

Traditional Loyalists and Mavericks

The typical Polish American politician in Buffalo, indeed the very stereotype of the ethnic machine politician, is the "traditional loyalist." The type does not include a clear majority of the leaders who were interviewed, but it covers a plurality, perhaps 40% to 45%.[37] Most GOP and many Democratic leaders fall into this category, although organizational loyalty among Polish Democrats seems to be of recent origin. Traditional loyalists are highly ethnic in their perceptions of politics and devoted to the party organization. They often hold (or have held) party office, work for the organization at election time and tend to individual requests from their constituents. Mostly they think of politics as a group struggle for recognition and individual patronage, a means of livelihood in fact for the many who hold public jobs. Issues or program related

---

[37]An exact calculation is impossible because of the leaders' impression of our measures of both party loyalty and, to a lesser extent, the ethnic vs. non-ethnic perceptions of political rewards.

matters are not important to them. Privately they may grumble over the lack of Polish recognition — the ex-mavericks particularly so. Publicly, they do not rock the boat.

Mavericks owe their survival to their popularity among Polish voters and to their skill in personally assisting constituents. They care little for issues or a politics that serves as a vehicle to advance the interests of their ethnic group in tangible ways. The political battle does not focus on what a Polish office holder does to improve schools, recreation facilities, police protection or public transportation on the East Side. Instead the battle is won or lost when a Pole is or is not nominated or appointed. The symbolic aspects of who acquires an office are more important than what is done with the power of the office.

The Respectables

Buffalo's Polonia, like other Polonia's has had some leaders who differed qualitatively from the loyalists and mavericks. These leaders, the "respectables" as they may be called, are increasing in number, particularly in suburbs. They represent perhaps a quarter of the contemporary leadership. Their background is more middle class than that of the others. Often they are college educated, and many possess a law degree. As third or fourth generation Americans usually, many have been so acculturated that their Polishness is confined to their name and sense of identity.

More importantly, the respectables differ greatly from loyalists and mavericks in their view of what is significant in the political process. They cannot ignore the politics of recognition, particularly when it may serve to their advantage. However, they are more inclined to emphasize issues, policy positions, programs and middle class virtues like honesty and efficiency. Respectables are likely to list specific laws, programs, administrative reforms or crucial judicial decisions when asked about their greatest achievements.[38] For many, politics is conflict over what is best for the entire city rather than between social groups. Some respectables are so assimilated that they are uncomfortable if not embarrassed about their ethnicity. They recognize the electoral advantages of their Polishness and are compelled to accomodate recognition politics to their world view since it is such a pervasive factor in Buffalo. But

---

[38] I asked each leader to note his/her greatest political achievement, hoping to discern ethnic and non-ethnic perspectives. This succeeded only partially since they gave multiple responses, some ethnic and some non-ethnic. Nevertheless, there was a positive relationship between class status and achievements noted. Middle class, younger leaders noted programs and issues; older leaders noted elections and appointments.

many wish the old system would go away, allowing their marginal status to evaporate and freeing them to focus entirely on issues like good "American politicians."

Figure 1 indicates that respectables are loyal to their party. This may be surprising. One expects such a middle class, assimilated group to incline toward the non-partisanship of the Anglo-Saxon ethos. Yet an examination of their background, attitudes and behavior demonstrates that this is rarely the case. Republican respectables have been party stalwarts for years. The more common Democratic respectables are a fairly recent phenomenon, in part the result of the influence of the Democratic county chairman. Joseph Crangle has recognized that a candidate with a respectable middle class image *and* an ethnic surname can appeal greatly to diverse blocs of voters, particularly in county contests where coalitions of middle class and ethnic voters are required. But the party expects a return for its endorsements, essentially a cooperative attitude on patronage, campaigns, fund-raising and support of other endorsed candidates. Some respectables have been required to serve in a party office as a kind of apprenticeship to being slated for an elective position.

The ties between the party and most respectables are so close that it is not surprising to discover that many rate party loyalty and service as an important or very important factor in their political careers. They are comfortable with the relationship. The party renders electoral support in exchange for loyalty and cooperation on patronage and intra-party affairs. Since the party seldom demands adherence to its line on public policy issues unrelated to elections and appointments, respectables are not forced to compromise their integrity on the matters which concern them most. This arrangement has proved so satisfactory and stable that one is tempted to suggest that more respectables will appear as younger, middle class Polish Americans are recruited into politics.

The Reformers

"Reformers" are perhaps the rarest of Polonia's politicians, constituting at most 10% of the contemporary Buffalo leadership group. Yet they are often the most articulate, controversial or well know personalities. They resemble respectables in their background and belief system. Usually they are third or fourth generation

Americans, middle class, college educated and acculturated. They also are oriented to issues and policies as political goals. Some share the respectables' ambivalence toward their ethnicity and ethnic politics generally. Others, however, have managed a coherent synthesis of ethnic and issue politics. Unlike the respectables, reformers are anti-party in their attitudes and behavior. They often describe both party organizations as "machines" and their leaders as "bosses". Refusing to accept party discipline, they frequently challenge endorsed nominees in primaries.

Reformers resemble mavericks in some respects. Both are anti-party and usually have a solid political base, enabling them to assume such an attitude with impunity. Yet there are crucial differences between them. Most mavericks are anti-party because they perceive the party as anti-Polish. Their traditional concern for patronage recognition leads them into independence. Reformers may criticize both parties for neglecting to recognize Polish Americans, but they dislike party structures and decision-making for ideological reasons even more. They consider party politics in Buffalo with its hierarchical structure, centralized decision-making and powerful chairmen to be undemocratic. No public constraints, they believe, exist to compel the parties to be more responsible and democratic. The true reformer really wishes to alter the very structure of party politics. Most mavericks would become loyalists if the county chairman was Polish and Poles were granted more recognition, but the true reformers would not be satisfied by such changes. As one of them noted: "a boss is a boss, whether he is Polish, Irish or Black. They're all out to take advantage of the public." His remark suggests another reformer value: that politics in Buffalo is and always has been corrupt; and that the "machines" are a major cause of this corruption. Furthermore, corrupt and unqualified leaders who hold power because of the machines hinder the formulation and implementation of necessary public policy.

To summarize, reformers are anti-party because (1) party politics is undemocratic and non-responsive; (2) parties promote dishonesty and incompetence; and (3) by so doing, parties prevent consideration of the real policy needs of a community. Alternatively, they wish to open party decision-making and require competence and honesty, as opposed to party loyalty, of all candidates for public office. Some would go so far as to eliminate party influence entirely by requiring non-partisan elections to city and county offices.

Conclusions

Many politicians would disagree vehemently, but an analysis of the politics of Buffalo's Polonia points first of all to a remarkable record of electoral success. At this writing the community is represented by a congressman, a county comptroller, more than ten state and local judges and several local and state legislators. Most significantly, it has produced three mayors, a record councilmen, county supervisors and, recently, county legislators have been elected by and represent fairly homogeneous ethnic of these is that Poles have taken advantage of their position as the largest ethnic bloc in the area through the cohesiveness of their vote and their willingness to support a co-ethnic even when it has meant crossing party lines. Furthermore, since 1927 at least, the local political structure has favored ethnic politics.[39] District councilmen, county supervisors and recently county legislators have been elected by and represent fairly homogeneous ethnic neighborhoods. The system has assured Polish Americans representation and given many leaders a secure base upon which to build political careers. Finally, the inclination of the Republican party to nominate Poles in order to win elections has been notably helpful in advancing Polish interests.

The second conclusion to emerge from this analysis is that despite numerous electoral victories, Polish Americans have never taken control of the local political system as, for example, the Irish have in New Haven, Boston, Chicago and, for that matter, in Buffalo. Inability to control party structures, particularly the Democratic, is both cause and consequence of this failure. The obvious reason is that Poles are only one of four or five other large ethnic groups in the area. A sizable Italian community, a growing black population and a "Wasp" (or German) constituency in the suburbs mandates coalition politics in order to win elections. Much less than a majority, the Poles simply do not have the numbers to take over. Besides, they may lack the skills and interests required to play the broker role demanded by coalition politics. A successful political broker must be flexible, adept at compromise, perceptive, sensitive to the legitimacy of claims by groups other than his own, and willing to work for and remain loyal to the party's decisions. Ideally, he should be able to point to a record of party fidelity among his voters. On the contrary, many Polish leaders have been not only anti-party,

---

[39]Gordon, "Immigrants and Urban Governmental Forms."

they have often led the opposition in party feuds. The ticket-splitting of Polish voters may elect Republican mayors and councilmen but it does not endear them to non-Polish Democrats. The fact that Polish leaders cannot always "deliver" their wards has hurt Polish interests within the Democratic party.

Why, one may ask, have not Polish Americans developed broker skills, and what has kept them from becoming party loyalists? Part of the answer may lie in a certain social personality. Though there are dangers in national character analysis, it seems true that many Polish Americans have found it psychologically difficult to compromise, particularly on issues that touch their group pride. Once convinced they are right, they will struggle for their position though the odds be clearly against them. Indeed, some leaders actually appear to glory in such behavior, preferring a good fight for what they see as a noble cause to the benefits of pragmatism. Some of the leaders interviewed for this study noted another and less romantic trait, using words like "jealous," "selfish," and "distrustful" to describe their peers. Perhaps this is only the obverse of the Polish desire to maintain a distinctive individuality. As one proverb has it: "Where you find three Poles, you find four parties." Whatever the cause, it appears that cooperation among Polish leaders in Buffalo, particularly over an extended period of time, has been rare.

By contrast, Polish leaders cite the example of Irish politicians as mutally supportive. They seem to possess as well the very skills that the Poles lack — flexibility, pragmatism, party loyalty and an eagerness to play the part of broker in the city's factional politics. Their recognition and cultivation of the growing importance of the black vote is but one sign of their pragmatism. Put quite simply, Irish skill more than Polish character deficiency has limited Polish power in local party politics. The mavericks may not be simply paranoid in their perception of the intentions of party leaders. Despite a declining Irish vote, Irish leaders have zealously maintained their influence by mobilizing coalitions against their major rivals — the Polish Americans. Understood thus, the Irish Democrats did not recognize blacks and Italians solely out of pragmatic considerations, but to forge a coalition to prevent the more numerous Poles from taking over the party. If indeed this has been the strategy of the last three Irish Democratic county chairmen, it offers another explanation of the Polish failure to assume control of the party.

The complex, varied nature of the political elite in Buffalo's Polonia should dispel simplistic notions of contemporary ethnic leadership. An unqualified distinction between old (and disappearing) ward leaders and younger, middle-class, acculturated leaders does not reflect the richness of the situation. Party loyalty, for one, complicates matters, and, more importantly, ethnicity continues to influence attitudes and behavior. The assimilation to a new American culture, symbolized and long-expected in the image of the melting pot, has affected some ethnic leaders not at all and many younger politicians in ways which were not anticipated. All politicians in Buffalo must come to terms with the pervasive ethnic life of the city. However, some respectables and reformers represent more than mere accomodation to the rules of ethnic politics. They have begun to synthesize ethnic and issue oriented conceptions of politics. As Glazer and Moynihan suggest, ethnicity has lately become more politicized.[40] Ethnic groups have mobilized politically throughout the world. Their demands are in part symbolic (i.e., the old game of recognition), but now often include tangible benefits for the entire group. Some Buffalo Polish leaders also want more than Pulaski Day parades, recognition and patronage, and they concern themselves with better schools and housing, cleaner air, the sensitivity of urban planners to community values and institutions.

The synthesis of issue and ethnic politics is surely a novel development. Young, third generation ethnic leaders do not necessarily become assimilated, public issue "Wasps." They may combine issue politics and ethnic demands to create a new style of leadership (and here we have a third major, albeit more tentative conclusion of this analysis), one which may mean the revitalization and redefinition of the salience of ethnicity in local politics. The appearance of issue oriented ethnic leaders also portends a new ethnic politics in Buffalo, one characterized by greater conflict. The old ethnic politics was a low stakes game: group demands for recognition, patronage and statues of national heroes, which could be accomodated with a minimum of strain on the local political system. Extensive redistribution of economic resources was not required since it was easier and less costly to give Polish Americans a political office than a neighborhood high school or hospital. If many more ethnic leaders begin to play a new game, the strains on

---

[40]Moynihan and Glazer, *Ethnicity*, pp.7-8. Some highly critical impressions on the political position of Buffalo's Poles are in Walter Drzewieniecki, "Status spoleczny i polityczny Polonii polnocnoamerykanskiej na przykladzie miasta Buffalo," in H. Kubiak and A. Pilch, eds., *Stan i Potrzeby nad Zbiorowosciami Polonijnymi* (Wroclaw: Ossolineum Press, 1976), pp. 282-302.

local political system, already beset by problems of crime, pollution, race relations and rising costs, will be immense. The only certainty is that the predictions of the end of ethnic politics must again be extended or at the very least revised in the case of Buffalo.

THADDEUS C. RADZIALOWSKI
with DONALD BINKOWSKI

Polish Americans in Detroit Politics*

The history of the Polish experience in Detroit has never been adequately chronicled. We have neither the close, continuous analysis of the voting patterns of Polish precincts over a long period of time nor good in-depth studies of the careers of Polish American political figures and their milieu that have been done for other cities. Our interpretation of the Detroit situation must therefore be based on analysis of more occasional data, and a greater weight must be placed on impressionistic information. Nevertheless, the available evidence clearly shows that the political, social and economic development of Detroit during the last one hundred years made the Polish immigrant political experience in the city distinctly different in important respects from those undergone in other centers of Polish settlement.

The Poles appeared in significant numbers in Detroit shortly after the Civil War. The first to come were a few skilled artisans, but they were soon followed by unskilled country people. The newcomers found work as laborers in foundries, stove works, railroad shops, construction and excavation, and as field hands on the farms of the Ferry Seed Company. In addition to work as stoop laborers for Ferry Seed, Polish women were employed mainly as domestics and cigar makers. Detroit at the time was just beginning the industrial expansion and remarkable growth that was to make it one of the largest and most important industrial cities in America by the 1930's. It mushroomed from over 45,500 in 1860 to 116,340 in

---

*We wish to thank the Immigration History Research Center of the University of Minnesota for the use of its facilities and collections, the generous assistance of its staff, and for a grant-in-aid which supported part of the research for this essay. Special thanks also go to Ms. Gloria Peters and Ms. Lisa Cariolano for their invaluable clerical and editorial assistance.

1880. By 1900, it had grown to 286,000 and reached about one half million inhabitants in 1914.[1]

The problem of determining the exact number of Poles in Detroit, as elsewhere, is complicated by the absence of a Polish state census and the practice of immigration officials in depending heavily on country of citizenship as a test of origin. Sister Remigia, the historian of early Polonia in Detroit, drew on a variety of sources to give the following estimates of the Polish population: 22,000 in 1885, 35,000 in 1892, 48,000 in 1900. The Detroit *Free Press* estimated 40,000 Poles in 1890. That same year, Henry Tillman, a major Republican strategist, counted Polish voters by wards and precincts and put the Polish voting strength at more than 25% of all those eligible. By 1914, Polish immigrants and their children numbered 110,000 to 120,000 and with almost a quarter of the population, were on their way to displacing the Germans as Detroit's largest minority group.[2]

The earliest Polish settlers in Detroit were from Prussia, Kashubes from the Baltic region and Poznanians. They settled next to the Germans, the group they knew best in Europe, and they initially used the ethnic institutions the Germans had established, especially the church. It was probably through contact with Catholic Germans and to a lesser extent the Irish, that the Poles in Detroit were originally introduced to the Democratic party. The Michigan Republican party had little attraction for the new immigrants. Its base was primarily the Protestant and rural population of the state, which had strong nativist and prohibitionist proclivities. In Detroit, the GOP was the party of native Protestants and especially of the economic and industrial elite.[3] The later Polish immigrants from Galicia and Russian Poland who settled next to Prussians on the East Side and founded a smaller settlement on the West Side of the city in the 1800's followed the pioneers into the

---

[1] For population see Donald R. Deskins, Jr., *Residential Mobility of Negroes in Detroit, 1837-1965* (Ann Arbor: University of Michigan, 1972) pp. 202, 256-59; Sidney Glazer, *Detroit: A Study on Urban Development* (New York: Bookman Assoc., 1965) pp. 36, 52, 107-8; and Sister M. Remigia, *The Polish Immigrant in Detroit to 1914* (Chicago: Polish Roman Catholic Union, 1946) p. 29. For information on the occupations of Polish immigrants see Deskins, pp. 75-76 and Sister M. Remigia, pp. 33-39. Sister Remigia's study provides a great deal of basic information on the early history of Detroit Polonia. Eugene Ostafin, *The Polish Peasant in Transition: A Study of Group Integration as a Function of Symbioses and Common Definition,* Diss., University of Michigan, 1948, is an excellent study of the early history of the East Side settlement with a sociological slant. The best available study of Hamtramck is Arthur Wood, *Hamtramck* (New York: Octagon Books, 1974). Wood emphasizes the more sensational aspects of Hamtramck politics and occasionally accepts his informants' information too uncritically. For a personal and highly interpretative overview see T. Radzialowski, "The View from a Polish Ghetto: Some Observations on the First 100 years in Detroit," *Ethnicity,* 1: No. 2 (Summer, 1974), 125-39.

[2] Sister M. Remigia, p. 30; Melvin G. Holli, *Reform in Detroit* (New York: Oxford University Press, 1969), pp. 11-12. The presence of more adult males in the Polish community than in the general population probably explains the discrepancy between the population estimates which set the Polish population at 12%-20% and the more than 25% of the eligible voters assumed by Tillman.

[3] On Michigan political parties see Holli, pp. 12-13; on the experience with the Germans see Ostafin, pp. 25-50.

Democratic party.[4] The first settlers with their better education, artisan trades, their familiarity with the Germans and their longer residence in the city were in the best position to act as leaders of the new community. Thus, a disproportionate number of Polish office holders in the period before World War I were Kashubes and Poznanians.[5]

By the last decade of the nineteenth century the Poles grew restive and resentful under the control of Irish and German political bosses who took their votes for granted. That restiveness translated itself into massive Polish defections from the Democratic party when the Republicans fielded an attractive candidate for mayor in the 1889 election. The GOP candidate, Hazen Pingree, conducted a successful personal campaign in Polish areas of the city and put a Pole on his slate. He came out in favor of the eight hour day and by opening his campaign at "Baltimore Red's" Saloon, he made it clear that he did not oppose the whiskey trade. Pingree won the election and carried the Polish districts by a greater plurality than he gained in the city at large.[6]

The Poles continued to support the Republican Pingree in the nineties while engaging in relatively sophisticated ticket splitting to vote for Democrats at national and state levels and for municipal offices other than mayor.[7] In 1896, when Pingree ran successfully for governor of Michigan, he won a majority in the Polish wards at the same time as these went strongly for William Jennings Bryan, the Democratic candidate for president. During Pingree's tenure as mayor, he won the affection of the Poles by his attacks on the high charges and monopolistic practices of the utilities, and the exorbitant rate hikes of the Detroit Railway Company. He fought for a working man's trolley fare and provided work, relief and small garden plots for the unemployed during the severe depression of 1893. No other important Republican figure was ever able to win from the Poles the kind of support they gave Hazen Pingree. Although his influence was, on occasion, strong enough to increase

---

[4]The West Side colony around the church of St. Casimir was founded by Austrian Poles and remained largely Galician. The East Side community was always the larger of the two Polish settlement areas. The East Side was the usual first settlement area of all immigrant groups and until the last great southern black migration, the "Catholic" side of Detroit.

[5]Among the Poles who held elective or appointive offices before 1914 are people with names such as Schmidt, Neubauer, Lemke, Welzand, Maior and Konkel, indicative of their origins in the northwestern Polish areas under German control. The first Pole elected to office was Felix Lemke, justice of the peace in 1876. In 1880, Adolph Jasnowski was elected to the state legislature. See Sister M. Remigia, pp. 59-61.

[6]Holli, pp. 18-21; Sister M. Remigia, p. 53.

[7]The sophisticated behavior of the Poles surprised the Detroit newspapers. The Detroit *Free Press* observed in 1895 that "the Poles seem to have found out how to split their tickets and voted for the Republican candidate for mayor and the Democratic candidate for alderman." The Detroit *Tribune* commented that "there seems to be an opinion that the Polish American is governed in the exercise of his franchise by a complicated set of rules which only he and a few experts understand and the motives which actuate others have little or no influence with him." Sister M. Remigia, pp. 53-54.

the number of votes other Republicans won in Polish districts, the Pingree interlude did not represent a serious inroad by the Michigan GOP into the Polish vote. During the entire period Poles continued to vote overwhelmingly for Democrats at all other levels. Thus, their votes for him recognized that as a maverick in his own party, he served their interests better than the candidates of their own party.[8]

After Pingree's retirement in 1900, the Poles reverted to that pattern of straight ticket support for the Democratic party which had prevailed prior to 1889. Indeed, it was in the years before 1910 that they created and accepted that particular blend of identities as Poles, Catholics, workers, Democrats, Americans and Detroiters which characterized their ethnicity in Detroit. Over time, this core of values continued to be shaped and modified by international, national and local events, by sometimes competitive and abrasive relationships with other ethnic groups and by local and national struggles within the Polish community. In some cases, the importance of certain identities, such as region of origin waned, while others such as union membership, for example, supplemented and enriched the evolution of Polish ethnic identity.[9]

The plural identities of Polish American ethnicity and the complex interests to which they were tied complicated politics for Detroit's Polonia from the very beginning. The issue was first posed most directly when the immigrants were forced to choose between voting as Democrats or voting as Poles. From its founding in 1904, Detroit's most influential Polish newspaper, *Dziennik Polski* (Polish Daily News) urged Poles to vote for Polish candidates regardless of party and to split their ballots when attractive non-Polish candidates ran on the GOP ticket. This was to serve notice on Irish and German bosses who "regularly forget about us after election" that the days of "beer barrel politics" and automatic

---

[8]Holli, pp. 70-72, 76-94, 102-6, 110-11, 193-96 and *passim*. During the Depression of 1893, 24,000 of 28,000 people on the poor rolls were foreign born. Polish and German workers accounted for more than 50% of the persons on pauper relief.

[9]Victor Greene, *For God and Country* (Madison, Wis.: The State Historical Society of Wisconsin, 1975), builds his argument around the importance of internal, communal struggles in the rise of group consciousness among Poles and Lithuanians. He concentrates primarily on an analysis of the battle between elite factions in the Polish community in Chicago and devotes little attention to Detroit. Greene has also made an interesting and partially successful first attempt to deal with the difficult problem of the coexistence of Polish and American identities in Polish American consciousness in his essay, "Slavic American Nationalism, 1870-1919," in Anna Cienciala, ed., *American Contributions to the Seventh International Congress of Slavists, Vol. III: History* (The Hague: Mouton, 1973) pp. 197-215. My approach differs from Greene's in suggesting that a sense of being Polish and a sense of being American were both a part of their ethnic identity and that this identity was also formed and reinforced by religious affiliation, class, and occupational factors, political allegiance, familial, neighborhood and parish ties, secular and religious society membership and town or city loyalty. As early as 1908, for example, *Dziennik Polski* carried extensive accounts of Detroit Tiger baseball games, which were apparently avidly followed by many of its immigrant readers. See also Arthur Kornhauser, *Attitudes of Detroit People Toward Detroit* (Detroit: Wayne State University Press, 1952), pp. 205 ff.

support for the Democrats were over.[10] These efforts by the newspapers and some community leaders were usually in vain. Polish Republicans running against non-Polish Democrats were decisively defeated with regularity in the Polish wards.[11] The staunch adherence of the Poles to the Democratic party was clearly manifest during the Republican landslide of 1904. Detroit and Wayne County went for the GOP at all levels except the Polish 5th, 7th and 9th East Side wards, which held for the Democrats.[12]

During the first decades of the community's existence, Poles in Detroit had at times responded to injustice, inequity and unemployment by violence, riot and the destruction of property. With their growing political strength by the turn of the century, they turned to the ballot box to redress grievances and win jobs. Polish voters for example, usually supported bond issues for public works projects such as the Detroit Museum of Art Building and the Belle Isle Bridge, aware that these would mean jobs. (This was prior to the full development of the automobile industry.)[13] During the 1910 election campaign, *Dziennik Polski* expanded its criteria for endorsement to include the willingness of an incumbent to hire Poles in any of the patronage positions available to him.[14] Most importantly, by 1910 the Polish community had become successful enough in electing some officials and placing others in public jobs to begin to engage in the politics of status and respect.[15] The Polish leadership, for example, waged a very successful campaign in 1910 to deny votes to Thomas A. Farrell, the incumbent County Clerk, because "he has nothing but disdain for Poles, treats them rudely and makes things very difficult for them when they are in his office." His behavior was contrasted with that of Charles Nichols, the incumbent City Clerk, who "respects Poles" and treats them "like first class citizens" and has even "gone out of his way to assist them if necessary." Nichols did surprisingly well for a Republican in the Polish wards while Farrell received fewer votes than any other candidate on the ballot in the same wards. At the same time, State Senator August Cyrowski, in a hitherto unprecedented move by a Polish office holder, broke publicly with the "Irish dominated"

[10]See for example, *Dziennik Polski,* October 8, 1904, for the 1904 election, and October 31, 1908, November 2, 1908 and November 5, 1908. It must be pointed out the *Dziennik Polski* leaned editorially toward the Republicans on national issues. See "Za kim Glosowac?" (For whom to vote?), August 23, 1904.

[11]In the 1910 election, M. Koscincki, running as a Republican against the German, Hindle, the Democratic candidate, lost the Polish 5th precinct in the 7th ward by a vote of 121 to 29. *Dziennik Polski,* November 10, 1910. The wards in which the greatest number of Poles were concentrated were the 5th, 7th, and 9th wards on the East Side and 16th ward on the West Side. Smaller numbers of Poles lived in the 3rd, 11th, and 13th East Side wards and the 14th and 18th West Side wards.

[12]*Dziennik Polski,* November 9, 1904. In the 9th ward a single Republican, an alderman, was elected. The 5th and 7th produced solid majorities for all Democrats.

[13]*Dziennik Polski,* November 3, 1910. For the 1908 election, on the same issue see *Dziennik Polski,* November 2, 1908.

[14]*Dziennik Polski,* November 1, 4, 1910.

[15]By 1908, there were three Polish aldermen: S. Skrzycki in the 7th ward, M. Ostrowski in the 9th and X. Konkel in the

leadership of the Democratic party. "It did not take me long to discover why (the Irish) scorn and mock us" he said, "because they think we will vote for them no matter what because we know no better. . ." He predicted that the scales would soon fall from the eyes of the Poles and they would recognize the true nature of those Irish "Pharisees."[16]

Although nothing so dramatic happened to Polish voters, there were changes in their community's self awareness which began to alter political interests and involvement. The first change, briefly alluded to, was an increased interest in the status of the community and the regard with which it was held by others in Detroit. On the eve of World War I, the Polish community in Detroit had been in existence for almost half a century, though it was still struggling to absorb a flood of newcomers. In that time many Poles had saved enough to purchase small homes; eleven parishes had been established and more than half of them had built large, impressive churches and parish schools. A Polish seminary for priests had been founded. A small professional class was beginning to emerge, and over 2,500 businesses run by Poles were in operation. In addition, with the advent of the new auto industry came a period of relatively secure employment and comparative prosperity for the laborers who formed the overwhelming majority of Detroit's Polonia. Unlike the "hungry nineties," the immigrants now could afford an interest in status and the politics of respect. This tendency was given reinforcement and content by two related developments. The first was a sense of conscious Polishness that had grown along with the ties that bound the immigrants into parishes, societies and areal communities and separated them from others, especially the nearby Germans. This consciousness was fostered by the efforts of newspapers, pastors of the Polish parishes and teaching nuns in the parochial schools, all of whom had an interest and commitment to community solidarity. Struggles between elite factions in the Polish community in Detroit and elsewhere over its nature, purpose and future also raised questions which forced many to define a clear identity. The new consciousness and the desire for status and recognition is well exemplified by the celebrations which attended the visits to Detroit of Chicago's Auxiliary Bishop Paul Rhode, the

16th. In 1904, only Ostrowski held a seat. In addition, August Cyrowski became the first Pole to hold a state senate seat. He was elected from the Third Senatorial District which covered the Polish wards of the East Side. Other Poles were elected constables and to other offices. A complete listing of those elected or holding an appointive position before 1914 is in Sr. M. Remigia, pp. 60-61. Konkel lost his seat from the West Side Polish ward in the 1910 election, thus reducing the Poles' total to two. *Dziennik Polski,* November 10, 1910.

[16]*Dziennik Polski,* November 1, 1910, November 4, 1910, November 5, 1910. The paper also noted other incumbents who treated Poles with respect.

first Polish American raised to the episcopate.

The second development was an increasingly militant Polish nationalism, spreading to almost all elements of the Polish nation and to the communities in diaspora. In the twentieth century the amount of money and energy American Poles devoted to the struggle to maintain Polish culture and language in America and help their European brethren win respite from the oppression of the partitioning powers increased significantly. The 1910 rallies and celebrations to commemorate the 500th anniversary of the Polish-Lithuanian victory over the Teutonic Knights at Grunwald, held in partitioned Poland and in Polish immigrant communities are testimony to the burgeoning national feeling. By 1910, *Dziennik Polski* and the organizational newspapers which Detroit Poles read increased significantly the amount of space they devoted to news and commentary on Polish matters. During World War I, such concerns began to dominate the newspaper columns and the almost miraculous reappearance of a Polish state between 1918 and 1922 seized the attention of Polish Americans to the virtual exclusion of all other interests. The emerging Polish state became a new and for a time, important point of reference for the immigrants and a symbol of their new status as a people with a state.[17] As a result, national and local political concerns received only passing notice by the Polish press into the early 1920's.

While the Poles were preoccupied with events in Europe, a package of "good government" reforms was passed which changed the nature of the political arena in Detroit to their decided disadvantage. The large aldermanic council which included two representatives from each ward was replaced by a nine member city council elected at-large in a nonpartisan fashion. The patronage available to elected officials was cut dramatically to only a handful of positions. Students of the wave of "good government" reforms in American cities at the beginning of the twentieth century have pointed out that they shifted the balance of power back to the upper classes. In at-large elections the strength of geographically concentrated ethnic and other minority groups was negated. The

---

[17]Indicative of this new self consciousness was a resolution passed by the Detroit Common Council at the insistence of the Poles which paid tribute to the Polish Americans in the armed forces and authorized the purchase of a Polish flag to be placed among the flags of other nations "in graceful tribute (sic)." This was more than thirteen months before the War ended and at a time when the Polish state was still but a dream. The same resolution was urged upon the county auditors in June, 1918. See Allan R. Treppa, "Chronology, 1913-1920," *The Citizen* (Hamtramck), October 20, 1977. During the 1916 elections the proclamation of a new "Kingdom of Poland" by the Central Powers on November 1 took most of the headlines and front page space away from national and local races. *Dziennik Polski*, November 1, 1916. In November 1920, Polish Americans had their attention riveted on the struggle over Wilno and the Upper Silesian plebiscite and only on Wednesday, November 3, 1920 did the papers note, almost in passing, Harding's victory. On the day before the announcement, election day, and the day after it, the front pages of the papers were full of news of the exciting events in Poland.

deceptively named "nonpartisanship" created by the reform shifted the organization of the campaign, the nomination of candidates and the definition of the issues from the political parties in which the immigrants were acquiring considerable influence to civic groups, "search light" and special issue committees, newspapers, reform groups, chambers of commerce, businessmen's alliances, booster clubs, and other organizations which middle and upper class people found more compatible and virtuous as vehicles for political participation.[18] It is perhaps not entirely coincidental that the "reform" of city government which culminated in the new charter of 1918 came at a time when the Poles had become the largest minority group in Detroit. That the reform had as one of its purposes the exclusion of the immigrants from political power is further evidenced by the fact that the same constellation of political forces responsible for the new charter was also involved in the passage of the 1894 Constitutional amendment which limited voting in city and local elections to US citizens.

For several reasons, Polish community reaction to these efforts was ambivalent. The war, the Polish national renaissance and the campaigns to collect food, clothing and money to alleviate the effects of war on a homeland in which friends and kin still lived, temporarily eclipsed interest in city politics and redirected energies from local concerns. Also, many Poles were not sorry to see humbled the arrogant and corrupt party bosses who took their votes for granted and gave them far less than their due. Indeed, Senator Cyrowski's public attack in 1910 on the Democratic party leadership marked the beginning of a two decade long erosion of Democratic party strength among the Poles. In the midst of increasing war prosperity and with the community now well established, the nexus of loyalties as immigrants, Catholics and workers which had brought the Poles into the party began to weaken. [19] In the 1916 election, for example, two of the four Poles elected to the Detroit Common Council were Republicans.[20] A

---

[18]On reform in Detroit, see William Lovett, *Detroit Rules Itself* (Boston: Gorham Press, 1930), *passim*. A similar reform's impact upon the participation of Pittsburgh lower classes is in Samuel P. Hayes, "The Politics of Reform in Municipal Government in the Progressive Era," *Pacific Northwest Quarterly*, 55 (1965), 157-69. The reform groups in Detroit were led by such luminaries as James Couzens, Henry Ford's righthand man, J. L. Hudson, Detroit's leading merchant, and the patrician, John C. Lodge. Their membership was concentrated in the brotherhoods of the downtown Protestant churches, the exclusive clubs, and the Anti-Saloon League. As part of the package of reforms, Detroit and Michigan voted prohibition in 1916, to take effect in 1918. Although the city itself voted wet, it was overwhelmed by a strong outstate vote against liquor.

[19]It is not known whether the powerful role the Germans played in the leadership of Detroit's Democratic party encouraged Polish defections after 1914. However, the Germans seemed to have begun defecting from the party sooner and in larger numbers than the Poles. See *Dziennik Polski*, November 10, 1910, for a comparison of votes for Republicans in the Polish and German precincts of the 5th Ward in the 1910 election.

[20]*Dziennik Polski*, November 9, 1916.

contributing factor to the erosion of Polish support was the moribund nature of the party itself. Beginning in 1894, the Democratic party in Michigan experienced a sharp decline in voter support that was not arrested until the Great Depression. As its latest recruits, the Poles were really among the last to begin leaving a party which had less to offer with each election while Republican power was growing apace.[21] By 1918, a significant minority of Poles had strayed to the Republican party whose leaders were in a vanguard of the urban reform movement in Detroit. Thus opposition to the reform movement, which was tied up with the defense of the existing Democratic ward machines, was blunted by a swing toward the Republican party.[22]

Another factor which was to have a profoundly distinguishing effect on Polish politics in Detroit was the settling of the village of Hamtramck by Polish immigrants. Hamtramck was a rural township north of the Detroit city limits on the East Side, inhabited by German and Dutch farmers and by a few roadhouse and saloon owners who supplied prostitution, gambling and other entertainments to Detroiters. The area began to change dramatically after 1910 for two reasons: it was just north of the border from rapidly growing Polish neighborhoods in the 9th ward, and it was chosen by the Dodge brothers as the site of their new automobile factory. The lure of jobs accelerated the movement of Poles from neighborhoods south of Hamtramck and drew in their kin and compatriots from as far away as the Pennsylvania anthracite fields and the upper Michigan copper mines. The Poles were accompanied into Hamtramck by much smaller groups of blacks, Italians and other Slavs, especially Ukrainians. Following the example of the Dodges, other auto makers built factories in Hamtramck as the industry expanded and this in turn pulled in more immigrants. By the early twenties, the Poles composed the overwhelming majority of the city's population. When the area was incorporated in 1922, the first mayor and a major part of the newly elected administration were Polish. Meanwhile, Detroit itself had grown rapidly around and beyond Hamtramck, making it (like Highland Park to the northwest, where Henry Ford's great plant was dominant) an enclave in the heart of Detroit's East Side.[23]

[21] Lovett, pp. 56-57.
[22] Certain Detroit Democrats, especially those in Republican wards favored some aspects of the reform, such as non-partisan elections. Lovett, pp. 57-58.
[23] There is a persistent belief among long time residents of Hamtramck that another reason the area was so attractive to the Poles was that the Dodge Brothers promised to keep the area "open," especially for liquor after prohibition passed in 1916, and free of the puritanical restrictions that Ford imposed on Highland Park. There is also a conviction among many in Detroit's Polish community that just as the majority of West Siders are Galicians so the bulk of those in Hamtramck are "Russians," i.e. Poles from the "Kingdom," the area officially under Russian control from 1815. There is no study which

The influx of newcomers and the establishment of the auto industry in Hamtramck did nothing to disrupt its first major industry—vice. In fact, the advent of new money and new customers only helped to foster it. When Hamtramck was still a semi-rural village its five trustees had run all the saloons, and graft and fraudulent elections had long been honored political traditions. When the Poles took over the political machinery in the twenties, they too were drawn into the pattern of official corruption and protection of brothels, gambling houses and illegal saloons. Vice in Hamtramck proved to be a remarkable example of inter-ethnic cooperation. During the Prohibition era a motley, polyglot collection of Irish saloon keepers, Jewish racketeers and brothel keepers, black and Polish gamblers, dishonest old stock American and German police officials and corrupt Polish politicians turned the city into Detroit's favorite playground. It also served to convince many in Detroit that the Poles were incapable of honest self-government, much to the dismay and confusion of the largely law abiding Polish population clustered around the remarkable churches being built in the residential clearings between the giant factories.[24]

The Hamtramck experience played a crucial role in the political history of the Poles in Detroit. The city's bawdy and tumultuous early years gave Poles a reputation, largely undeserved, as an ungovernable people and confirmed for many the old stereotypes and prejudices long current in Detroit that Poles were barely capable of civilized life. That the vice, liquor and gambling in this "Polish City" were mostly in the hands of others, and that the attacks on Hamtramck by Detroit newspapers and various police agencies smacked heavily of stereotyping, went largely unnoticed.

In spite of its unsavory reputation, however, most Poles, whether they lived in Hamtramck or not, took considerable pride in the idea of a "Polish City." The election of the pharmacist Peter Jezewski as the first mayor of the new city of 48,000 people in April, 1922 led to prolonged celebrations in the Polish community. No Pole had ever attained so high a municipal position. The end of village status, supported by the Poles as a weapon against the entrenched village establishment, and the victory by Jezewski came in the wake of the municipal reform, which had curtailed the political power and representation of Poles in Detroit. Hamtramck

substantiates this belief. Besides the Poles among the newcomers, only the blacks and Ukrainians were to play a role in Hamtramck politics. The blacks constituted a small but sometimes important swing vote and black ministers were always among the leaders of the regular campaigns against gambling and prostitution.
[24]Wood, pp. 46-114.

was compensation for losses in Detroit. Its discrete boundaries, political offices and patronage provided far more visibility and rewards than control of four or five Detroit wards could ever have given, even in the pre-reform period. It gave Detroit's Polonia a manifest physical location and uncontested control over a piece of the urban landscape. Hamtramck's Poles met with high state and federal officials and corporation chiefs; they taxed, built schools, named streets and zoned property. Elsewhere important decisions were made for them by others; in Hamtramck, Poles controlled their own destiny. Hamtramck officials became important figures in the Polish community and among its most important spokesmen outside of it. As a result, the city attracted a large share of the community's intelligensia, professionals and many ambitious and able would-be leaders who saw a greater possibility of using their talents and winning rewards and recognition than in Detroit. In the thirties, Hamtramck became the arena for a Polish American radicalism which would have been diffuse and certainly lost from sight in the wider Detroit scene. The existence of Hamtramck, a city composed of Polish American workers, was also crucial to organizing the East Side automobile factories.

Finally, since the city broke the political unity of the massive Polish East Side settlement and attracted potential leaders and voters, its existence also had a negative effect on the political development of Detroit's Polonia. The number of registered voters in Hamtramck between the mid-thirties and the mid-fifties remained constant at about 24,000. Such a total would not be decisive in a mayoral race in which 150,000 to 250,000 votes were likely to be cast, except in a very tight contest. However, 15,000 to 20,000 votes were of considerable importance in at-large common council races in which primary nomination and election to one of the nine seats were often decided by a handful of votes.[25] The appeal of Hamtramck to capable young leaders also reduced the potential number of good Polish candidates for Detroit city offices.

During the 1920's, the Poles, who made up about 20% of the population managed to place only one of their members in an important municipal office. This was John Kronk who emerged as a Republican candidate from the 16th ward prior to the elimination of party labels in city elections and who later held one of the nine council seats during the period. The most interesting development in the 1920's was the rapid withdrawal of the Poles from the

[25]In the 1957 primary election, for example, 20,000 votes separated the third place from the tenth place and two of the three Polish candidates would have finished in the top nine with an additional 20,000 votes. *Detroit News,* September 11,

Democratic party. In the 1924 election the only Pole elected to the state legislature was the Republican, Jozef Bahorski. In the 1926 election four Poles, two state representatives and two state senators, all Republicans, were elected. In Hamtramck, the vote for state representative was 1,632 for the Republican Jozef Dziengielewski to 308 for his Democratic opponent. In the 1928 elections, the number of Poles in the state legislature declined to three, two Republican state senators, George Kolowich and Cass Jankowski and one state representative, a Democrat, Albert Bielewski from Hamtramck. Bielewski was the only member of his party sent to the legislature from Wayne County. (His Republican opponent lost by 300 votes out of the 7,011 cast. His name was Thaddeus Machrowicz, and he later represented the First Congressional District as a liberal Democrat.) In the national election, the Poles, voting as Catholics, wets and immigrants, gave the Democrat Al Smith a three to one margin over Herbert Hoover in Hamtramck and equally impressive if slightly smaller margins elsewhere.[26]

The Smith candidacy in 1928 marked the beginning of the end of the two decade erosion of support for the Democratic party among Detroit Poles. The phenomenon was strongest in Hamtramck, but it seems to have occurred in all Polish areas. In the 1926 election, the Republican congressional candidate carried Hamtramck by a more than five to one margin; two years later the Republicans lost the seat. In the second state senatorial district, which included much of the Polish area south of Hamtramck, the Republican Jankowski won by a three to one margin in 1926. He was barely re-elected in 1928 by a 252 vote margin out of more than 35,000 cast. In the third state senatorial district which included Hamtramck and the surrounding area to the north the Republican margin was almost six to one in 1926. It was reduced to little more than two to one in 1928 and the Republicans failed to carry the Hamtramck part of the district.[27]

The 1920's also saw the election of the first Pole from Detroit to the United States Congress. By chance, a young Polish politician, John Sosnowski, was nominated the Republican candidate in the First Congressional District, which included the Polish East Side. Riding the Republican tidal wave of 1924, he swamped his Democratic opponent Robert Clancy by over 40,000 votes to

1957. It should be pointed out here that as the West Side settlement expanded westward, Poles moved into the north end of Dearborn and then back into Detroit. In Dearborn, however, the Poles never played a role of such significance as they did in Hamtramck, since they were not as numerous.

[26]On Machrowicz, who rose to become a Congressman and a federal judge, see Marek Swiecicki and Rόza Nowotarska, *The Gentleman from Michigan,* translated by Edward Cynarski (London: Polish Cultural Foundation, 1974).

[27]On the election results see *Dziennik Polski,* November 1, 1924, November 3, 1906, November 7, 1928.

become, after Kleczka of Milwaukee and Kunz of Chicago, the third Pole to serve in the United States Congress. His tenure was limited, however, to one term. The idea of being represented by a Pole, even if he was a Republican, was too much for many Detroiters to swallow. In 1926, Sosnowski was defeated in the Republican primary when Clancy, his former Democratic opponent, switched parties and won the right to run in the general election as the Republican candidate, a victory which was then tantamount to election.

Although it is clear that by 1926, the Republican party had succeeded in winning over a substantial number of Polish voters, the size of the Republican margins among them was inflated by the failure of a very large number of Poles to vote. A strong and consistent pattern of voting by a very large percentage of the Polish population did not become a political characteristic of the Poles in Detroit until after 1932.[28] In the second state senatorial district, for example, the number of votes cast in 1924 was about 9,000, 6,000 in 1926, and 35,000 in 1928. In 1928, the vote split almost evenly between the Democratic and Republican state and local candidates. In Hamtramck, slightly less than 2,000 voted in 1926 while over 7,000 (out of 8,345 registered voters) cast ballots in 1928. That it was Democrats rather than Republicans who were likely to stay home is attested to by the 1930 election in which the Republicans won back the seat they had lost in 1928 by a vote of 2,421 to 1,637. Yet, in 1930, there were 14,000 registered voters in Hamtramck.[29]

If Smith's candidacy halted the Democratic slide among the Poles and reactivated many who still supported the party but had lost faith in it for becoming impotent and increasingly irrelevant to their concerns, then the Depression and the union organizing struggles of the 1930's brought almost all Detroit Poles back into the fold. By the mid-thirties, the Poles had become the single most important bloc of voters in the Detroit Democratic party. The Polish areas in that period consistently produced the largest number of straight-ticket voters for the party—in some precincts as high as 94 percent.[30] Having entered the New Deal Democratic party forged by Franklin Delano Roosevelt, the Poles of Detroit became its most

[28] Donald S. Hecock, *Detroit Voters and Recent Elections* (Detroit: Detroit Bureau of Governmental Research, 1938) p. 6. Hecock concludes on the basis of his study of four elections in the mid-1930's that "the sections of the city most consistently leading in the proportion of registered voters participating were the Polish precincts just north of the Michigan Central tracks in wards 16, 18, and 20 and those bordering Hamtramck . . ." Edgar Eugene Robinson, *They Voted for Roosevelt: The Presidential vote, 1932-1944* (Stanford, California: Stanford University Press, 1947), marks the 1936 election as the campaign in which the Eastern and Southern European ethnics began going to the polls in massive numbers. The turnout in cities with large immigrant populations in 1936 was double that of 1932. In those cities in which the workers were of Northern European origin, the increase in 1936 over 1932 was small.

[29] *Dziennik Polski*, November 5, 1930.

[30] Hecock, pp. 10-11. The only areas of Detroit with an almost equal proportion of straight ticket voters were the

loyal supporters at the national level. FDR was given majorities of 90 to 94 percent in the Polish areas of Detroit. Although his Democratic successors never attained the same pluralities, they garnered large majorities in Polish districts through the 1970's. Truman, Kennedy, Johnson and Hubert Humphrey all received 80% or more of the vote in Polish neighborhoods, Stevenson won almost 80% while McGovern and Carter, whom the Poles found less congenial, each received about 60% of the vote in areas such as Hamtramck. Though there is no specific study of the maintenance of ties to the Democratic party by Detroit Poles who have moved into adjacent suburban areas, it is probably safe to assume that the majority remain Democrats. The areas in which they have been concentrated invariably return Democratic majorities in partisan elections.

As a result of their return to the revitalized Democratic party, a large number of Poles appeared on the party ticket in 1932. In that year, after decades of estrangement from the seats of political power, three Polish Americans were elected to Congress from the Detroit area: George Sadowski from the East Side's First Congressional District, and John Dingell and John Lesinski from the Fifteenth and Sixteenth Districts on the West Side. Three of the six Detroit seats were occupied by Poles until 1964 when the congressional districts were redrawn. Two of the three were then re-elected (in the new First and Sixteenth Districts) and continue to hold those seats to this day. Their control of half the congressional seats in Detroit from 1932 to 1964 and of two of six since 1964 represents the most powerful political position the Poles have attained in Detroit. These seats and their geographical concentration also gave the Poles a great deal of leverage in the local Democratic party, which in Wayne County is organized by law by congressional district. In addition, local branches of the AFL-CIO Committee on Political Education (COPE) are organized on the same basis and play a pre-eminent role in partisan politics. The Polish American hold over party machinery was the strongest on the East Side in the First Congressional District.[31]

wealthiest residential areas on the West Side (Bretton Drive and Southfield Road) and those bordering Grosse Pointe (Indian Village). The straight ticket votes were cast, of course, for the Republican party. Black areas in the 1935 election cast the highest proportion of straight Republican tickets, but in 1936 they began to shift to the Democrats. The blacks with their historic ties to the Republican party were among the last of Detroit's working class groups to come into the New Deal coalition.

[31] George Sadowski won in a special election in 1932 to the 1st District seat. His election was a harbinger of the coming Democratic sweep. Sadowski and Rudolf Tenerowicz held the 1st District seat in the 1930's and 1940's and were succeeded by Thaddeus Machrowicz who, in turn, was followed after his appointment to the federal bench by Lucien Nedzi, the present Congressman. Dingell and Lesinski were both succeeded by their sons and namesakes in their respective districts. In the redistricting of 1964, the two were pitted against each other and the more liberal, Dingell, with strong UAW support, won the seat which he continues to hold. J. David Greenstone, *Labor in American Politics* (New York: Alfred A. Knopf, 1969) pp. 115-16, 125-26, 196, 259, 291-92.

Several powerful factors combined with the successes of Polish Americans on the party ticket to tie them to the Democratic party. The first was the impact of the Depression. When the great crash came, the Poles were only in the first stages of a painful climb toward a minimum standard of security and home ownership. As one of the poorest and least skilled ethnic groups in the city they dropped back to poverty and joblessness in large numbers in 1929-1930. At the height of the Depression almost half of the 11,000 families in Hamtramck were on relief. City resources were stretched so thin that by 1933 families with fewer than three children were taken off the relief rolls. Not since the severe Depression of 1893 had Detroit's Polish population suffered such privation.[32] New Deal relief programs were seen as salvation by the sorely beset Polish community in Detroit and solidified its grateful adherence to the Democratic coalition. To Poles, Roosevelt became the man who rescued them from the slow death of unemployment, the horror of bread lines and soup kitchens and the humiliation of relief. The 700 jobs the WPA provided in Hamtramck provided the Democratic party with more than a generation of loyal supporters among the city's Polish workers. As a direct result of the Depression and the New Deal, there was a massive shift of Poles to the Democratic party. Former Republican party activists and even candidates and office holders withdrew from the GOP and surfaced shortly afterwards as Democrats, sometimes bitter and disillusioned that their former party was so unconcerned about the plight of Polish workers.[33]

A second important factor promoting Polish adherence to the Democratic party was the massive involvement of the Poles in the struggle for unionization in Detroit, especially among auto workers. The battle united almost all elements of the Polish community in defense of the interests of the workers for the first time since the pre-World War I period. Between 1936 and 1942, the majority of Polish American politicians appeared regularly at workers' meetings and rallies. Merchants donated food to sit-down strikers and various necessities to the families of workers. Labor organizers spoke regularly on Polish radio programs. A Polish conference of assistance and solidarity was created by a variety of patriotic, social, political and benefit societies. During the bitter Ford strike in 1941, a conference manifesto described the issue as a

[32]Wood, p. 56. Caroline Bird, *The Invisible Scar* (New York: David McKay, 1966), p. 33. The situation was so severe that candidates for constable in Hamtramck hoped to win the homeowner vote by promising to conduct evictions in a humane manner. In Detroit, allowances fell to 15 cents a day per person before they ran out completely.
[33]Interview by Donald Binkowski of Adam B. Kronk, April 2, 1974.

struggle of all of American society "but in particular, Polish American (society)" for democracy. Henry Ford was characterized as an associate and supporter of Adolf Hitler and the underwriter of all fascist organizations in America. Victory over Ford, the manifesto concluded, was necessary to safeguard the gains of workers at all other factories. This remarkable manifesto was signed by two congressmen, a state senator and a state representative, a Hamtramck city councilman and a judge, and the presidents of the Polish Citizens Central Committee, the Polish Women's Alliance of Michigan, several Polish National Alliance branches, Group 8 of the Polish Roman Catholic Union, the Polish University Club, the Polish Lawyers Association, a citizens club of a Polish parish and other organizations, as well as by radio personalities, newspaper editors, individual lawyers and Polish UAW organizers and officers of locals. It represented the complete spectrum of opinion from right to left in Detroit Polonia.[34]

This kind of community support not only made organizing Polish workers easier in Detroit than elsewhere, it also helped to encourage and legitimize the strong representation of Polish workers in the grass roots leadership of the spontaneous workers' uprisings that accompanied the organization of the UAW and other Detroit unions, such as the cigar workers.[35] There is no question that without the Poles, the largest minority group in most of the auto factories, the organization of the UAW and other unions would have been impossible.[36] In turn many Polish workers

[34]Stanislaw Nowak, "Wklad Polonii Detroickiej w organizowanie robotników fordowskich," *Glos Ludowy* (Detroit), October 8, 1977. Nowak was the major Polish organizer for the UAW in the Detroit area and later a state senator. His memoirs, serialized weekly in *Glos Ludowy* and running for over two years, are a major source for the study of the unionization of Polish workers in Detroit. Aside from an occasional politician and the *Dziennik Polski*, the major opposition to the unions came from some of the pastors of Polish parishes. Also see Stanislaw Nowak, "Udzial Polaków automobilowych w USA," *Problemy Polonii Zagranicznej*, VI—VII (1971), 165-89; Peter Friedlander, *The Emergence of a UAW Local, 1936-1939* (Pittsburgh: University of Pittsburgh Press, 1975). The parish priests were probably more interested in maintaining their influence with their parishioners than they were in supporting the claims of the capitalists. Many workers were, however, simultaneously parish leaders and union activists without apparent difficulty. Nowak reports that he often heard workers tell him that "In religious matters, I follow the pastor; in work matters, I follow Nowak." Stanislaw Nowak, "Próba zlamania strajku w zakladach McCormicka" *Glos Ludowy*, November 12, 1977.

[35]Stanislaw Nowak, "Polonia a ruch unijny," *Glos Ludowy*, November 5, 1977. Nowak feels that the Polonia support was much stronger in Detroit than elsewhere. Comparing Detroit with Chicago he writes, "In every case the work of organizing there (Chicago) was much more difficult than in Detroit." In Chicago, for example, Polish workers were unable to get on any of the Polish radio programs to plead their cause and spread the union message. Nowak, "Próba zlamania . . ." Friedlander notes that the importance of "community organizations cannot be overestimated, for the communal aspect of the organization of the Polish workers seems to be one of the most important characteristics of the UAW in Detroit." Friedlander, pp. 4-5.

[36]Nowak, "Udzial Polaków . . ." A similar case can be made for the organization of the CIO in general. Over 600,000 Poles joined the CIO and they were the largest minority in key industries such as steel, auto, agricultural machinery, coal mining and meat packing. Without their support the unions in those areas would have been crippled or destroyed. On this see Boleslaw Gebert, "Polacy w amerykańskich zwiazkach zawodowych: Notatki i wspomnienia," *Przeglad Polonijny*, II, Part I (1976), 151-64. Boleslaw "Billy" Gebert was an organizer for the steel workers union. According to Friedlander, the leadership of the movement seems to have come primarily from second generation Poles. The first president of the UAW paid tribute to the important role the Poles played in organizing the UAW in a letter to *Glos Ludowy*. He wrote: "Polish workers in the battle with General Motors showed that they were the most progressive and militant workers in the country." In Nowak, "Udzial Polaków . . .," p. 188. The sitdowns of the mainly Polish women cigar workers and their heroic

acquired organizational skills and a political orientation by participating in the union movement. When the UAW moved into the Michigan Democratic party in the 1940's, many Poles became party activists primarily as a result of their union ties and often as UAW-COPE workers. For Detroit Polonia as a whole, with its preponderance of union workers, the union local became an extension of the community and especially of its political and economic aspirations. Union locals supplemented and even displaced to a degree the political club and the parish as an entree to political patronage.[37]

The city of Hamtramck also played an important role in the politics of unionization. On the one hand, the independent existence of the city as an enclave in Detroit was due to the influence of the Dodge brothers, as Highland Park owed its creation to Henry Ford. The company (which was merged in the 1920's into the Chrysler Corporation) paid a large share of the city's taxes and exerted considerable power over the day-to-day operation of the municipality. Its watchdog was the Hamtramck Board of Commerce, whose secretary in the 1930's, Fred White, was the hand picked representative of Chrysler President K. T. Keller. The corporation, for example, managed to have taxes it found too heavy rescinded in the late 1920's and through its creature, the Board of Commerce, the Corporation in 1933 engineered the dismissal of the welfare director, Mrs. Trojanowski, who was considered too liberal.[38] The Chrysler Corporation used the ever-present threat that it would relocate and take tax money and jobs out of Hamtramck, as Henry Ford did in Highland Park, to keep the municipal administration docile. When the organizing in Hamtramck began, the Corporation expected the loyalty and support of the city administration.

On the other hand, the fledgling Dodge union also saw the importance of controlling the city administration and the largely proletarian character of the city's electorate made this a real possibility. In 1936, with the assistance of the union and a radical People's League, of which more will be said later, a pro-labor administration was elected. After the election, the new city attorney announced that "the police will not protect strikebreakers in Hamtramck. The city is neutral."[39] When the Dodge strike came,

resistance for over three months in early 1937 appear to have sparked a wave of strikes and sitdowns among the thousands of women in Detroit who worked as store clerks, office workers and in other service jobs.
[37]Friedlander, pp. 100, 127. On p. 145, he notes that "the broader involvement of the mass of Polish workers caused the union administration and the Democratic party machine of Hamtramck to become intertwined in the formation of a hybrid political machine, complete with patronage."
[38]Wood pp. 63-64; *Newsweek*, March 6, 1937, p. 9.
[39]*Newsweek*, ibid.

the police actually helped the sitdowners close and secure the Hamtramck doors of Dodge Main while Detroit police escorted strikebreakers through the back entrances in Detroit. They also handled with care and consideration the crowd of over 10,000 who gathered to prevent a rumored attack by militia or state police. In a strike at a General Motors plant, they formed a cordon at the city line to prevent state forces being brought into the city for use against the strikers. The natural sympathies of the policemen had free play because one of the Dodge local unions (number 3) had handpicked the police chief after the 1936 election. The mayor and members of the council appeared often as speakers at workers' rallies and one, Mary Zuk, took part in the strikes herself. In spite of continual deficits and the constant threat of bankruptcy, the city made it a practice during several administrations to hire Chrysler Corporation strikers for occasional labor even in excess of appropriations.[40] In this process, the local Democratic party, the nonpartisan city administration and Dodge Local number 3 of the UAW were fused in an unusual but effective organization. In spite of occasional rifts the coalition has held.

The political awakening of Polish workers in Detroit in the 1930's also had a radical tinge to it which left a mark on their political orientation. Early labor struggles and the onset of the Great Depression caused some Poles to move to the left of the Democratic party by the 1930's. In addition, a small but not insignificant group of immigrants had had previous experiences with socialism in Europe.[41] The deepening depression, increased labor strife and growing political consciousness led to the development of a strong leftist tendency in Polish politics in Detroit. Polish Americans were among the leading organizers of the march of the unemployed in 1932 which was dispersed by police gunfire at the Ford Rouge plant. One of the four who died in the massacre was a young Polish organizer and march leader, Joe York (Jurkiewicz), and several other Poles were among the wounded.[42] In Hamtramck, a People's League was organized which successfully ran candidates for the city council, organized housewives' boycotts of merchants whose prices were too high and drummed up community support for the unions.[43] Even though the People's

---

[40] Wood, pp. 68, 77; interview with S. Nowak, June 16, 1977.
[41] Friedlander, pp. 21, 100, suggests about 10% had some socialist sympathies as a result of an urban industrial experience in Europe prior to emigration.
[42] Nowak, "Udzial Polaków . . ." p. 165.
[43] Wood, p. 62. The People's League called for increased relief; no police interference in labor disputes; an end of racial, religious and ethnic discrimination; a prohibition on the use of labor spies, armed guards and black lists; an end of gambling and vice; repeal of the sales tax; construction of recreation centers, playgrounds, libraries, hospitals, clinics and public toilets; preference to local contractors for city work; repeal of state sales tax; union wages on public projects; and a free city

League and especially the colorful Mary Zuk, member of the city council and boycott organizer, were often denounced as communists in press and pulpit, the radical movement in Polish politics did not disintegrate until the beginning of the Cold War. In the 1942 election, the communist George Kristalski managed to place eighth in the race for the five Hamtramck Council seats. In 1938, the popular radical journalist and labor organizer, Stanley Nowak was elected as state senator and held the seat for ten years in spite of attempts to remove him because of his alleged membership in the Communist party.[44]

Thus, events in the 1930's and 1940's caused a basic re-crystallization of the collection of characteristics that composed Polish self-identity in Detroit. To be Polish was to be a worker, a union member and a labor Democrat. The intertwining of labor unions and the Democratic party with ethnic political aspirations strengthened and fostered this identity configuration. The association of the merger of those elements with the recovery from the searing poverty and unemployment of the thirties caused most Polish Americans to view its maintenance as essential to their well-being into the 1960's, and many continue to see it in that light to the present.[45]

Having tied themselves to the labor-Democratic party coalition, the Poles in Detroit shared its success in partisan politics. They also shared its failures in nonpartisan city elections and were indeed partly responsible for some of those defeats.[46] An important reason for the failure of the Detroit unions to elect their candidates was the nonpartisan system which allowed the diverse and sometimes antagonistic ethnic and occupational groups in the labor-Democratic party coalition to splinter and vote other interests free from party discipline. At the local level the Poles, as home owners, voted as fiscal and social conservatives, while in state and national elections they cast their ballots for liberal and socially progressive candidates.[47]

employment bureu. In the 1936 election, Mrs. Zuk was the only League member elected, but the mayor and two other councilmen were also pro-labor.

[44]Wood, pp. 81, 94. One study regards Poles as the most "militant" and class conscious of Detroit's white workers. See John C. Leggett, *Class, Race and Labor: Working Class Consciousness in Detroit* (New York: Oxford University Press, 1968), pp. 114-15.

[45]I can attest to the deep emotional tie to unions and to the Democratic party from personal experience. A sophomore in high school, I returned home from school the day after Eisenhower defeated Stevenson in 1952 to find my father hunched in a chair dejectedly and my mother sitting on the edge of a chair nearby weeping softly. When I asked the problem, my mother replied, "They won, now there's going to be another depression." My father, a rubber worker who was a veteran of the organizing period in the 1930's, said, "With the Republicans in, the bosses are really going to get down on us."

[46]On the unions' failure to elect their candidates, see Greenstone, pp. 110-40.

[47]Poles in Detroit, as elsewhere, resumed the purchase of homes after the Depression on a massive scale. The insecurity of the Depression years combined with the traditional attractions of home owning for the Poles may have accelerated the process. Poles as a group had a disproportionate tendency to own real estate. Edward O. Laumann, *Bonds of Pluralism: The*

With their strong position in the labor-Democratic party coalition and their geographical concentration, the Poles did well in county, state and national elections, but they were unable to elect many of their own to Detroit city offices. Only three Poles have sat on the Detroit City Council in the sixty years since the reform: John Kronk who was elected in the 1920's and served again briefly after World War II; Leo J. Nowicki, former Michigan Lieutenant Governor, who resigned during his first term to take over the troubled Detroit Street Railway system; and the public servant and accountant Anthony Wierzbicki, who served eight years until his defeat in the November, 1977 election.[48] For only one short period, after the 1948 election, did Detroit Polonia have two representatives on the nine member Common Council. The Poles on Detroit's council had certain common characteristics that distinguished them from most of the other Poles elected in Wayne County: little or no connection with the labor-Democratic party machine; a tendency to be fiscal and social conservatives; and the backing or endorsement of business and commercial groups, home owners or taxpayers associations, the Civic Searchlight or other good government organizations and/or the powerful *Detroit News*.

Only one Pole, Roman Gribbs, has ever been elected mayor of Detroit. A lawyer with a reputation as a fair, honest, and efficient administrator, he had been installed as Wayne County Sheriff to clean up a corrupt and scandal ridden department. His success led to his nomination for mayor, and he won a narrow victory over Richard Austin, the first black candidate for mayor of Detroit. Gribbs, who had a good civic rights record, ran an exemplary campaign, scrupulously avoiding any racial appeals in a city frightened and polarized by the memory of recent riots. He had, however, a limited interest in partisan politics, and after one term (1969-1973) of an administration that got high marks for solid and efficient if somewhat low-keyed achievement, he chose not to run

Form and Substance of Urban Social Networks (New York: John Wiley and Sons, 1973), p. 166. An interesting instance of political schizophrenia occurred in 1964 when the 15th and 16th Congressional Districts were merged and John Lesinski, Jr. was forced to run against John Dingell, Jr. Lesinski had been one of the few northern Democrats to vote against the Civil Rights Act of 1964, a decision which had been expected to enhance his appeal in an ethnically homogenous area inhabited by owners of small homesteads and threatened by black migration from the central city. Yet the election went to Dingell. Greenstone, p.126. The Polish vote for the liberal George McGovern(60%), which was higher than the vote he got from college professors (57%), also testifies to their continued willingness to vote for left-liberal state and national candidates.

[48]Leo J. Nowicki, an immigrant, was a graduate of the University of Michigan and the first registered Polish American civil engineer in Michigan. He was elected Wayne County Drain Commissioner during the Democratic tide of 1932. In 1936, he was elected Lieutenant Governor in a very tight race to become the first Pole to attain so high a state position (a second Pole, T. John Lesinski, has held that post for one term since). He lost narrowly in 1938 and missed a chance to become Governor, as the newly elected Governor, Fitzgerald, died in office shortly after his inauguration. He served as state budget director under Governor Van Wagner until he resigned to take a commission in the Transportation Corps in 1942. After World War II, he returned to work on the staff of the Detroit City Planning Commission. When he ran for political office again in 1948, he no longer had close ties with the Democratic party. He received strong support from the business community and Detroit newspapers in his successful campaign for Common Council.

again. The first Pole to hold that office, therefore, was succeeded as mayor of Detroit, a city over fifty percent black in 1974, by Coleman Young, the first black mayor. Gribbs was subsequently appointed to a judgeship.[49]

Any evaluation of the political experience of the Poles in Detroit must take into consideration two profoundly important factors: intense and bitter competition between the Polish and black communities; and deep, persistent prejudice, directed against Poles by better established groups in Detroit. The two factors have reinforced each other and embittered the competition. The geographic — social mobility and the political success of blacks has threatened the gains of Poles, who have felt held down by established groups. The struggle between the groups, especially in recent times, has been interpreted largely on the basis of an American experience which assumes that the economic and social competition can be explained only as part of a three hundred and fifty year old pattern of racist oppression of blacks by a dominant white society. Such casting of Poles in the role of oppressive "racists" absolved the Detroit establishment of the need to take their claims seriously and simultaneously legitimized and excused the existing prejudice against them.[50]

The competition between Poles and blacks in Detroit did not begin in earnest until the 1930's, and even then it was not always as total and continuous as it has been remembered through the filter of recent events. The relations between the two groups who shared the bottom of Detroit's society with southern white migrants—the so-called "hillbillies"—was at times marked by tolerance and cooperation.[51] Poles and blacks actively cooperated in politics in both Hamtramck and Detroit (the first black to run for the Detroit Common Council, Charles Diggs, ran on a joint ticket and campaigned with a Pole) and in the 1930's they formed the core of the New Deal coalition in the city. They also worked side by side in

---

[49]Gribbs sometimes received criticism from some segments of the Detroit community because he did not "do enough" for Polonia or did not appoint enough Poles to patronage posts. However, because of the 1918 reforms, the mayor has less than 50 patronage appointments and most of those require specialized knowledge and experience. Gribbs feels that if he had chosen to run again, his chances of being re-elected were excellent. However, he chose not to run because the position took too much time and energy away from family life and because he wished to return to his first interest, the law. Interview with Roman Gribbs June 17, 1977. On Gribbs' political style and his reputation as a "private" man and low key administrator who operated in an "incredibly businesslike manner," see L. Yourist, "Gribbs remains a Puzzle," *Detroit News*, December 31, 1973, 9-A.

[50]Most commentators have recognized only the first part of the problem and not the second. For example, Robert Shogan and Tom Craig, *The Detroit Race Riot* (Philadelphia: Chelton, 1964), p. 19, write, "The Poles, looked down upon by the more established nationality groups in Detroit, took out their resentment against Negroes, whom they regarded as a threat to the economic gains they were struggling to make." For my comments on these two factors and their relationship see my essay in *Ethnicity*, 125-50.

[51]Kornhauser, p. 13, notes that 6% of his Detroit sample felt the city would be improved by the removal of "foreigners," 13% would deport blacks and 21% considered the "hillbillies" as the most undesirable.

the automobile factories, often in the least desirable jobs, such as those in the foundries. The Poles were frequently the key to identifying the black leaders in a given department and to organizing the black workers, since they generally preceded the blacks into the union movement.[52]

On the other hand, conditions in Detroit also pitted blacks and Poles against each other for jobs, homes, status and political power with disastrous consequences. From their first appearance in large numbers in the industrial plants, the blacks presented a clear threat to jobs and higher pay. They were widely used and cynically exploited as union busting scab labor, especially during the organizing struggles in the 1930's, by Detroit capitalists, most notably Henry Ford. On occasion, armed by the company and at its instigation, they battled Poles and other ethnics on the picket lines during the organizing strikes. In attempting to move out of their overcrowded neighborhoods, the blacks encountered the tightly knit parish communities created by the Poles. Unlike other groups, the Poles did not readily give way and flee to distant all white neighborhoods. They had invested too much too recently in churches, schools, institutions and community to move. Detroit was for the most part a new city. It had not experienced, as had many eastern cities, the procession of groups through houses and neighborhoods, which tacitly legitimized and sanctioned the idea of temporary possession and succession. The Poles were living around churches they had recently built in neighborhoods that had been created out of raw pasture. They defended turf and community against outsiders who shared with them neither language and culture nor religion.[53] During World War II, as Detroit expanded and available housing disappeared, the two communities battled with clubs, knives and fists over control of a housing project until the blacks, who needed the housing more desperately and for whom it was intended, were moved in behind National Guard bayonets.[54] The following year, during the 1943 race riot, the fighting between Poles and blacks was renewed in a number of areas. While the struggle for jobs and the contest over

---

[52]Stanislaw Nowak, "Polacy i murzyny," *Glos Ludowy*, November 19, 1977. Also interview with S. Nowak, June 16, 1977. See also Lawrence Carter, "Poles, Blacks Won Harmony in '32 Election," *Detroit News*, May 4, 1975. Carter is a prominent black leader and columnist in Detroit. His column is devoted to his memory of Polish-black cooperation in the 1930's.

[53]Radzialowski, 134-37. Deskins, p. 107.

[54]This was the Sojourner Truth Project in Detroit's East Side. See Deskins, pp. 140-41; Shogan and Craig, pp. 29-31. The federal Office of Facts and Figures (OFF) investigated and cited a shortage of housing and hostility between Negroes and Poles as a major source of racial tension.

neighborhoods has never reached the violent proportions of the 1940's, it has remained a central issue is Detroit.[55]

Black-Polish rivalry has had an important political dimension if only because the two groups make up such a large proportion of the population of Detroit. Their geographical proximity puts them in the same political space and thus increases the competition. It is an unfortunate fact that to increase their political representation and their influence in the Democratic party, the blacks have had to reduce the power of the Poles. This situation has often led those who wished to break up the Democratic political coalition to make blatantly racist appeals, as was notably the case in the 1943 and 1945 municipal elections.[56] The rivalry has also been a major factor in shaping the political strategy of the unions. They entered the Michigan Democratic party, at least in part, to protect the union-ethnic coalition and to keep Detroit ethnic groups focused on economic and social issues. This involvement has encouraged the emergence of generally progressive candidates from the Polish community. The nonpartisan nature of Detroit city politics has, on the contrary, reduced the union coalition strategy to near impotence.

Anti-Polish feeling in Detroit derives from both anti-working class feeling and ethnic prejudice. Detroit has been marked historically by sharp division and antagonism between the working class and those above it, and the Poles, as one of the largest identifiable segments of Detroit's proletariat, have been the target of this upper and middle class prejudice.[57] The Poles have also been the victims of a strong and specific anti-Polish prejudice on the part

---

[55]Although there is no evidence that Poles played, in any sense, a central role in the Detroit race riot, the commander of the federal troops in Detroit noted the bitter feeling between "Negroes and the young hoodlum element of the Polish population" and the fact that this "element " harassed and even threatened to attack his troops for intervening in the riots. *Ibid,* p. 88. In some districts, police put the blame on gangs of "Italians and Syrians" and still others on "Southerners." Alfred McClung Lee and Norman Humphrey, *Race Riot* (New York: Octagon Books, 1968), p. 81. It appears that the rioters, black and white, represented many segments of the Detroit population.

[56]C. O. Smith and S. B. Sarasohn, "Hate Propaganda in Detroit," *Public Opinion Quarterly,* X (1946-47), 24-52.

[57]The upper and middle classes began to flee Detroit to escape the immigrant working class masses early in the 20th century to the North Woodward area and east to the Grosse Pointes. As a result, Detroit by 1930 was one of the most proletarian of cities. Interestingly enough this also seems to have been the case for immigrant groups. Detroit foreign-born groups in 1930 had smaller elites than in other large cities. On this see R. D. McKenzie, *The Metropolitan Community* (New York: Russel and Russel, 1967), pp. 122-23, 182-84. Class homogeneity and ethnic discrimination ironically have functioned to hold the Polish community together. See Leggett, p. 20 Leggett, a sociologist, a decade ago still described the Poles in Detroit as a "semi-marginal" working class group with rates of unemployment higher than other white groups. *Ibid.,* pp. 107, 219. Detroit Poles rank in the lowest one-fifth on the Duncan Index of Socioeconomic Status based on occupation. Only "Anglo Baptists" and "Not Affiliated Protestants" ranked lower among the 15 white ethno-religious status groups. The lower two groups presumably contain a large number of southern white migrants, the despised "hillbillies." On these see Laumann, pp. 191-95.

of Detroit's establishment from the beginnings of large scale migration to the city.[58] Part of this unfavorable image came as a result of the fact that they were a large group of rural, Catholic, peasant migrants, whose language and culture were strange if not bizarre to most Detroiters. In addition, they early acquired a reputation as a violent, troublesome people. The church riots within the Polish community in the 1880's were followed by work riots in the 1890's. On several occasions during the Depression of the 1890's, gangs of Polish workers attacked and drove off Italian workers at construction projects and took over the work themselves. In the most serious incident, the Conner's Creek massacre of 1894, Polish laborers who were dissatisfied with a reduction in wages attacked the supervisor and a sheriff's posse with shovels and then turned against all well-dressed people in the area. The posse emptied its pistols into the mob before it was overwhelmed. The riot cost three dead and at least fifteen wounded. The fear that the Poles inspired was illustrated by an editorial in the *Michigan Catholic,* the official newspaper of the Detroit diocese, which called for severe punishment of the "savage mob" of "howling Poles" and warned that the American people would not stand for their violence.[59]

The better inhabitants of Detroit did not easily forget or forgive the behavior, the lack of education, inability to speak English and low status of people who were threatening to take over their city. Officially, they ignored them. For example, George Catlin's massive 764 page history of Detroit published by the *Detroit News* in 1923 failed to make a single reference to a group which then numbered almost 25% of the population of the city.[60] When they could not ignore the Poles, they deliberately excluded them from positions of responsibility and visibility and kept them

---

[58] William Bunge, *Fitzgerald: The Making of a Revolution* (Cambridge, Mass.: Schenkman Publishers, 1971), p. 38, writing about the development of a neighborhood community on Detroit's West Side at the beginning of the 20th century notes: "while the prejudice against Poles, Gypsies, Negroes and Indians was intense, other prejudices tended to melt." Leggett, pp. 109-15, found in his Detroit study in 1966 that the majority of the black, high-status white (German and Anglo-Saxon) and Polish respondents agreed that next to blacks, Poles were the least likely group in Detroit to be invited to join a Gross Pointe club (blacks 59%, high-status whites 60%, Poles 51%). Blacks had a view of the Poles as having a lower status in the broader society than the Poles accorded themselves.

[59] Holli, pp. 66-68. The *Michigan Catholic* of course had no reason to love a people who just a few years earlier had forced Bishop Foley from his home in a church dispute. Polish workers also played a central role in the riots against the Detroit City Railway Company in 1891. These views of the Poles were probably reinforced by the prominent role played by Poles in sitdowns, picketing and street confrontations with the police during the tumultuous thirties.

[60] George Catlin, *The Story of Detroit* (Detroit: The Detroit News, 1923). Catlin was the librarian of the *Detroit News.* The situation had not improved significantly fifty years later. In a 1970 survey of textbooks one author noted, "The heavy Polish contribution to the building of Detroit is ignored . . ." Bunge, p. 191.

out of the better neighborhoods.⁶¹ It was not until 1962 that the last vestiges of the so-called realtor's point system was eliminated by the Michigan Supreme Court. The system was designed to keep blacks entirely out of Grosse Pointe neighborhoods and to screen out all but the most desirable Jews, Italians, and Poles.⁶²

As a result of the undisguised distaste and condescension many Detroiters have felt toward them, Poles have responded with sullen withdrawal and suppressed rage that contains strong elements of class hate and nationalist paranoia. After decades of Hamtramck jokes and anti-working class prejudice, Detroit Poles have, in spite of considerable political success in state, county and national elections, a sense of themselves as a suffering and persecuted people, a people without power or influence, which affects their political vision. This view was probably best expressed by the popular Polish language columnist, Mieczyslaw Lewandowski in the *Hamtramck Citizen* column in which he commented on the meaning of the Gribbs election. It has dawned on the city fathers, he wrote, that their policies have prepared a disaster for the city and they must now find a way to escape the responsibility for "the coming crises." "In such a situation, wise and prudent men seek a 'scapegoat' on whose innocent shoulders can be placed the responsibility for the atonement of the sins of others—for example, on a Negro or a Pole who will then have to answer before the electorate, when the expected social disorder and the looming crises comes upon us."⁶³ Part of this sense of powerlessness may come from the failure of Polish Americans to exercise any significant control over their local political environment, an important consideration for a people with a very local and personal view of power and community.⁶⁴ Their failure in this regard is the result of the success of Detroit's Protestant elite in "reforming" the city so that it remained substantially under its control until the present. That control is now

---

⁶¹The paucity of Poles in Detroit executive suites is notorious. The unions are not much better. In spite of the heavily Polish membership of the UAW and the key role played by Poles in creating the union, there is only one Polish American UAW International Representative at Solidarity House, the Union's international headquarters in Detroit. Until after World War II, Polish women had to change their names to German or English names in order to get positions as sales clerks in fashionable Detroit department stores such as J. L. Hudson. Women who did not hide their Polish identity could aspire only to lesser posts such as cleaning women. Only one Pole ever became a high school principal in the entire history of the Detroit school system. On this phenomenon in Detroit see Radzialowski, 140-41; and Martin Marger, *The Force of Ethnicity: A Study of Urban Elites* (Detroit: Wayne State University Press, 1974).

⁶²William Buffalino, "From Screening to Rule 9—to Fair Housing Laws," *Ethnic Communities of Greater Detroit* (Detroit: Wayne State University Press, 1970), pp. 200-7.

⁶³*Hamtramck Citizen,* November 13, 1969.

⁶⁴According to the 1970 census, foreign-born Poles and their children made up 14.2 percent of the population of the Detroit Metropolitan area. The addition of third and fourth generations would probably double the figure.

passing into black hands.[65] A secondary cause is the failure to develop enough talented politicians who had both an ethnic constituency and the broad community appeal necessary for success in the nonpartisan arena. The most talented Polish politicians were attracted to state and national level offices and partisan politics and two of the ablest politicians who chose the Detroit arena—Nowicki and Gribbs—quickly left it for appointive positions which offered greater stability and security of tenure than elected office.

[65]Greenstone, pp. 137-138, sums up very well the nature of the reformed Detroit system and its social and political implications for working class ethnic groups such as the Poles: "the imposition in Detroit of a nonpartisan political system with at-large city council elections . . . by Detroit's Protestant elite early in the century made it difficult for working class and ethnic minority groups to attain symbolic recognition through winning elective office or later, favorable policies on public housing and the like . . . In these respects Detroit local politics notably diverged from the partisan ethnically oriented systems of all the other very large eastern and midwestern cities with large European and Black immigrant populations. By comparison with other American cities, Detroit presented an extreme case of both the economic grievances that Marx emphasized and the sense of exclusion from the political community that concerned Bendix."

DONALD E. PIENKOS

The Polish Americans in Milwaukee Politics

Since the end of the nineteenth century, Polish Americans have comprised a significant portion of the population of Wisconsin and have ranked as the state's third largest white ethnic group, after the Germans and the Scandinavians. Since over half of all the Poles who migrated into Wisconsin settled in its largest city, Milwaukee, they have made the Cream City one of the most heavily Polish American centers to be found in the country.[1] Nonetheless, despite their numerical significance, and as I will show, their widespread participation in local politics, the Polish Americans have received little more than passing notice in studies of the city's politics. Even the renewed interest in the "unmeltable ethnics" shown by scholars during the 1960's and 1970's has largely ignored the Polish Americans of Milwaukee. For instance, only one, as yet unpublished, doctoral thesis has focused on the early history of the Milwaukee Polish community, or Polonia; and it was limited to the years before 1918.[2] Two assumptions guide this study: (1) that ethnicity remains an important factor in American urban politics, particularly in eastern seaboard and middle western cities of the United States; and (2) that ethnic politics differs greatly from one urban context to another, given the impact of the varying rules that govern political activity and the "ethnic mix" to be found in each city, among other factors. That both of these assumptions seem to be firmly grounded is clear from a reading of earlier research conducted in New York, Chicago and New Haven, Connecticut.[3]

---

[1] In 1900, 242,777 of Wisconsin's population of 2,069,042 were German-born immigrants. There were 61,575 Norwegians, making them the state's second largest immigrant group, followed by the Poles who numbered 31,882. In 1930, the state counted 2,939,006 residents, 128,269 of whom were Germans and 42,359 Poles. Norwegians, Swedes and Danes together numbered 66,293 persons. *Abstract of the Twelfth Census of the United States, 1900* (Washington, D.C.: Government Printing Office, 1902); *Fifteenth Census of the United States, 1930* (Washington, D.C.: Government Printing Office, 1932).

[2] Anthony Kuzniewski, "Faith and Fatherland: An Intellectual History of the Polish Immigrant Community in Wisconsin, 1838-1918," Harvard University Ph.D. Thesis, 1973. Additional background information about the political history of Polonia was furnished by conversations with a number of individuals who are knowledgeable about the local scene. I am particularly grateful to the following persons: Frank Zeidler, Clemens Michalski, Thaddeus Pruss, Francis Swietlik, John Polakowski, John Kalupa, Edmund Choinski, Stanley Budny, Harold Jankowski, John Plewa, Szymon Deptula, Anthony Szymczak, Edward Tomasik, and Philip Tuczynski.

[3] For example, Nathan Glazer and Daniel Patrick Moynihan, *Beyond the Melting Pot* (Cambridge, Mass.: M.I.T. Press, 1963); and Alex Gottfried, *Boss Cermak of Chicago* (Seattle: University of Washington Press, 1962).

Some Historical Background

The first Polish inhabitant of Milwaukee arrived as early as 1842, followed by a stream of immigrants from the German controlled territories around the western Polish town of Poznan. In 1866, the Milwaukee Poles formed their first parish, St. Stanislaus', on the city's South Side, and by the 1880's the Polish immigration was increasing rapidly.[4] According to the 1890 Federal Census over nine thousand Polish immigrants were living in Milwaukee, and one estimate of the total number of persons of Polish origin made at the time placed their population at about thirty thousand. Already the Poles had become the second largest ethnic group in the city. By 1906, the Polish population had increased to 70,000 persons, or 22% of the city total of 313,000. In 1955, the Polish Americans were believed to number 120,000 persons in a Milwaukee of 640,000 inhabitants. However, for over a century, an absolute majority of the city's population has been German or of German ancestry, a fact of decisive importance in understanding the possibilities of political success for Milwaukee's Poles.

The rapid development of the Milwaukee Polonia made it an early rival of Chicago, although immigration into Wisconsin declined markedly after 1900. Illustrative of Milwaukee's early dynamism is the fact that the first Poles in America to win the major political offices of state senator, city comptroller and US congressman were all from Milwaukee. The first successful Polish language daily newspaper in the United States, *Kuryer Polski* (The Polish Courier), was founded in Milwaukee in 1888. Two Polish fraternal insurance societies, the Polish Association of America and the Federation of Poles in America, were established in Milwaukee. The Kruszka brothers, Michael (1860-1918) and Wenceslaus (1868-1937), one a newspaper editor, the other a priest, became nationally known and influential figures throughout the American Polonia. In 1883, the Polish National Alliance held its fourth convention in Milwaukee and for several years afterward, the Alliance's organ, *Zgoda* (Harmony) was published there although its business office remained in Chicago. As early as 1895, fifty-five Polish societies and

---

[4]For the early history of the Milwaukee Polonia, see Thaddeus Borun and John Jakusz-Gostomski, eds., *We The Milwaukee Poles* (Milwaukee: Nowiny Publishing Company, 1946), particularly pp. 1-64, 111-27; Wenceslaus Kruszka, *Historya Polska w Ameryce* (Milwaukee: Kuryer Publishing Company, 1905, 1906), parts 3, 5, and 6; Bayrd Still, *Milwaukee: The History of a City* (Madison: The State Historical Society of Wisconsin, 1948).

organizations were in existence, a number that had increased to over one hundred by 1910.⁵ Two Milwaukee Poles, Michael Blenski (1862-1932) and Francis Swietlik (born in 1892) rose to national prominence as censor of the Polish National Alliance, at the time the highest office in that fraternal benefit society. In 1934, Swietlik headed the American delegation to the second World Polonia Congress in Warsaw, Poland.

Table 1. The Total Number of Polish Immigrants in Four Leading American Cities between 1870 and 1930: Some Comparisons

Polish Immigrant Population in:					Ratio of Milwaukee Immigration to:		
Census	Milwaukee	Chicago	Detroit	Buffalo	Chicago	Detroit	Buffalo
1870	325	1,205	285	135	27%	114%	241%
1880	1,790	5,536	1,771	723	32	101	248
1890	9,222	24,086	5,331	8,879	38	172	104
1900	17,033	59,713	13,631	18,830	28	125	90
1920	23,060	137,611	56,624	31,406	17	41	73
1930	19,593	149,622	66,113	26,616	13	30	74

Geographically, Milwaukee's Poles settled almost entirely in two districts within the city. The larger comunity was to be found on the South Side and included about three-fourths of all Polish Americans in Milwaukee. This settlement in 1924 covered a land area of roughly four square miles within which Poles made up at least 50% of all the inhabitants. In this district the organizational life of Milwaukee's Polish Americans was concentrated: thirteen Polish Roman Catholic and Polish National Catholic parishes, numerous fraternal insurance lodges (including the two that had been established in Milwaukee), numerous Polish-run businesses and banks, and the community's two Polish language dailies.⁶ A major industrial area, the Polish South Side community housed the powerful Milwaukee Social Democratic political movement. Under the leadership of Leo Krzycki (1881-1966) and Walter Polakowski (1888-1966), the Polish socialists enjoyed real success in the years between 1910 and 1932.⁷ Far to the north, along the Milwaukee River is a second and smaller Polonia whose members have huddled

---

⁵Kruszka, part 3, p. 126; Still, pp. 268-72. Gwen Schultz, "Evolution of the Areal Patterns of German and Polish Settlement in Milwaukee," *Sonderdruck aus 'Erdkunde' Archiv fur Wissenschaftliche Geographie*, Band X, 1956, Bonn, 139. Michael Kruszka's ideas are summarized in Edmund Olszyk, *The Polish Press in America* (Milwaukee: Marquette University Press, 1940), pp. 20-25.

⁶Borun and Jakusz-Gostomski, pp. 3-61; 167 ff.; 217-18; Schultz, 139-40.

⁷Donald Pienkos, "Politics, Religion, and Change in Polish Milwaukee, 1900-1930," *Wisconsin Magazine of History*, 61 (1978), 179-209.

together in the neighborhoods surrounding three Catholic parishes beginning in the late 1860's. The Polish Americans in this district were never as heavily concentrated in numbers as on the South Side, nor was their organizational life as intense.[8] One study of the names of Milwaukee registered voters found that in 1924, Polish Americans made up less than sixty percent of the electorate in the six most heavily Polish precincts on the city's North Side, compared to nearly seventy percent in the eighteen Polish precincts on the South Side.

Table 2. The Polish Electorate, 1924*

	North Side Precincts	South Side Precincts
Number of Precincts where over 50 Percent of the Voters were Polish Americans	6	18
Total Electorate in the "Polish Precincts"	3,926	11,682
Pct. Polish American	59.2%	69.5%
Number of Precincts where over 25 Percent of the Voters were Polish Americans	9	24
Total Electorate in these Precincts	5,673	15,661
Pct. Polish American	49.1%	59.6%
Number of Precincts where over 10 Percent of the Voters were Polish Americans	10	31
Total Electorate in these Precincts	6,323	20,212
Pct. Polish American	45.2%	49.5%

*In 1924, voter turnout in the Milwaukee mayoral election was 131,913. The city was then organized into 242 precincts.

[8] The first North Side Polish parish, St. Hedwig's, was established in 1871. A third Polish community, again with its own organizational and parish life, was located in the industrial towns of Cudahy and South Milwaukee, south of the city. According to census data presented in one recent study, persons of Polish stock comprised the largest single white ethnic group in five villages and cities south and southwest of Milwaukee: Cudahy (6.1% of the population), St. Francis (5.8%), South Milwaukee (5.0%), Franklin (4.2%), and Oak Creek (3.3%). In all the other five southern suburbs but one, West Milwaukee, Poles were the second largest ethnic group. In none of the northern suburbs did the Poles rank as high. Frances Beverstock and Robert Stuckert, *Metropolitan Milwaukee Fact Book: 1970* (Milwaukee: University of Wisconsin Extension and Milwaukee Urban Observatory, University of Wisconsin-Milwaukee, 1972).

Class, Religious and Political Characteristics

Milwaukee's Polish Americans have belonged largely to the working class of the city's population, having migrated to the United States with little in the way of formal education, arriving without knowledge of the English language, and originating mainly from rural Poland. A census taken in 1905, for example, revealed that 58% of the workers residing in Milwaukee's two most heavily Polish wards were unskilled, compared to 30% of the city's total work force. Conversely, while 13% of Milwaukee's employed population held proprietary and professional positions, the same was true for only 5% of the persons in the Polish wards. Given the fact that so many Poles had emigrated from the heavily industrialized German-ruled partition, it is likely, however, that at least some had experience in factories and machine shops prior to their arrival in America. Numerous Polish-owned shops and businesses were established, several of which eventually took their place among the largest family-owned firms in the state. Two of these are the Superior Die Set Corporation, owned by the Janiszewski family and Maynard Steel Company, owned by the Wabiszewski family. The emergence of a small yet influential business class within the Milwaukee Polonia as early as the first decade of this century served further to reinforce the Polish community's conservative ethos, a characteristic originally given it by the Polish clergy. Gradually, and particularly after the Second World War, large numbers of Poles and their descendants moved into skilled laborer and white collar occupations, and thousands have relocated their families in neighborhoods outside of the original Polonia boundaries, particularly in suburbs lying to the south and west of the city.

Before 1910, Polish American voters overwhelmingly favored the Democrats, although Kruszka's *Kuryer Polski* had adopted a progressive Republican orientation in 1900. In 1910, the Milwaukee Socialists elected their mayoral candidate for the first time and a sizeable Polish American vote was cast in favor of the new party's slate, which included one Pole, Martin Gorecki, running as an "at-large" candidate for alderman. In the Fall, 1910 statewide elections, another Polish American socialist named Michael Katzban was elected to the assembly from a district that included two heavily Polish South Side wards. Thereafter, until 1938, the Polish socialists remained an important part of the political scene in the South Side Polonia, although they never achieved any success on the North Side. Active trade unionists such as Gorecki, Katzban,

Krzycki, Polakowski and others made up a political leadership at odds with the clergy and businessmen, and until the Great Depression (when the Milwaukee Socialist party largely disintegrated), the Polish Americans in the movement were frequently successful candidates for elective office. Since 1928, when a Catholic, Al Smith, ran for president the Polish Americans have voted for the Democratic candidate for chief executive, even in those years when Republicans such as Eisenhower and Nixon won by landslide margins.

Table 3. Presidential Vote in Milwaukee and its Polish Wards, 1900-1976*

	Pct. Democrat	Pct. Republican	Pct. Democratic City-Wide Total
1900	59	34	40
1904	38	31	27
1908	49	23	37
1912+	34	21	39
1916	54	18	44
1920	24	39	18
1924+	16	28	10
1928	77	17	55
1032	80	7	67
1936	88	7	78
1940	84	16	64
1944	81	19	62
1948	76	24	61
1952	64	36	52
1956	56	44	47
1960	71	29	62
1964	75	25	70
1968	59	30	56
1972	57	39	56
1976	65	35	62

*City wards 12 and 14 between 1900 and 1922; wards 8, 12, 14, and 24 from 1912 to 1930; wards 8, 11, 12, 14, and 24 between 1932 and 1952; wards 8, 11, 12, 14, 17, and 19 between 1956 and 1968; and wards 8, 12, 13, and 14 for 1972 and 1976. Data derived from Sarah Ettenheim, *How Milwaukee Voted* (Milwaukee: Institute of Governmental Affairs, 1970) and *The Wisconsin Blue Book,* 1973 and 1977.

+The Socialist Eugene Debs won a plurality in the 1912 election; in 1924, the Progressive candidate, Robert M. La Follette, Sr. won a majority in the Polish wards and the city as well.

The overwhelming majority of Polish Americans has been Roman Catholic and only three small parishes of the schismatic

Polish National Catholic Church (founded in 1903 in Scranton, Pennsylvania) have been formed. The first and largest of these, Holy Name parish, was established in 1914 on the South Side. Originally, the clergy provided much of the leadership within Polonia because of its role in establishing churches and schools in the Polish neighborhoods. Probably the most influential figure during the formative years of the Milwaukee Polonia was the Reverend Hyacinth Gulski (1850-1911), who organized three different parishes during his career. Later, priests such as Boleslaus Goral (1876-1960), editor of the pro-Catholic and Democratic *Nowiny Polskie (Polish News)* and Wenceslaus Kruszka, whose half-brother Michael owned the *Kuryer Polski*, gained great influence within Polonia because of their connections with the two widely-read newspapers. Two Polish American clergymen, Edward Kozlowski and Roman Atkielski have served as auxiliary bishops in the Milwaukee archdiocese. Politically the Polish clergy generally favored the Democrats, whose party traditionally had been identified with Catholic immigrants. This stance placed them in agreement with the Polish business and commercial establishment.

Organizationally, the Milwaukee Polonia's development has paralleled that of other urban Polish settlements. A huge number of fraternal societies have operated in the community, providing their members with social contacts in addition to insurance protection. These groups have coexisted with the many parish associations characteristic of the Polish churches. In 1929, an "umbrella" organization named the Casimir Pulaski Council was set up to coordinate the activities of the many Polish groups and to serve as a pressure group in local politics. A second federation of organizations, the Wisconsin Division of the Polish American Congress, was formed in the mid-1940's with headquarters in Milwaukee. The Wisconsin chapter is part of the national Polish American Congress (itself established in 1944) whose purpose is to shape public opinion on issues concerning the Polish Communist government. For many years, the Pulaski Council, although a sizeable federation of groups in its own right, was also a member in the Congress and many individuals were active in the affairs of both organizations. Neither group has been very active in local politics in recent years, although their officers continue to participate at various civic ceremonies as recognized Polonia leaders. For example, both the president of the Pulaski Council and a vice president of the Polish American Congress were among the guests at a luncheon meeting with President Gerald Ford when he visited Milwaukee in March, 1976.[9]

Three succeeding "generations" of political leaders of the Milwaukee Polonia can be readily identified. Initially, between the 1870's and up into the early 1930's, the then essentially immigrant community was dominated by members of the Roman Catholic clergy, a few professionally trained individuals, including several newspapermen, with some competition coming from socialist oriented Polish trade unionists after 1910. The major issues confronting Polonia in this era coupled with the political styles of various leaders made the period particularly dramatic. Highly-charged ideological issues, ranging from the status of the Polish clergy in the Roman Catholic hierarchy to socialism and Poland's independence occupied the political attentions of the new Polonia. Equally important was Polonia's hunger for political influence within the Milwaukee community. For example, Michael Kruszka switched his newspaper's allegiance from the Democrats to La Follette's progressive Republican faction in 1900 because the city's mayor, a Democrat, had allegedly broken his promise to appoint the expected number of Poles to local government posts.[10]

In its second stage of development (from the 1930's to the early 1960's), American-born Polish politicians emerged in increasing numbers as Polonia's representatives. The struggle for political recognition was largely realized in these years; in the late 1940's and through the mid-1950's Polish American visibility in local government reached a peak. By then, six aldermen sat on the city's common council, two Polish Americans held judgeships, a large contingent of Polish Americans served in the state legislature and in county government, and the South Side possessed an already entrenched and popular Polish American congressman. Numerous federal appointive offices were held by Polish Americans, including Milwaukee's directors of the Federal Housing Authority, US Post Office, and marshal. Polish Americans also occupied several administrative posts in city government and in the police and the

---

[9]In May, 1977 a new, largely American-born group of activists was elected to lead the Wisconsin Polish American Congress. Dominating the organization's Board of Directors, these individuals have pursued a more active role in Polonia affairs than had been true in years. Among the Congress' initiatives was a successful effort to pressure the University of Wisconsin-Milwaukee to establish Polish studies course offerings at the college level; an agreement with local Jewish organization leaders to cooperate in areas of mutual concern, particularly anti-defamation and support of Soviet and East European human rights proponents; denunciation of the activities of the local Nazi party; and revitalization of the organization's statewide membership. (In early 1977, the Congress included thirty-one organizations. In March, 1978, it numbered forty-one member groups.) The changing character of the Polish American Congress also produced some tensions which led the Pulaski Council to withdraw from the still small "umbrella" group in May, 1978.

[10]The story of this period can be found in Donald Pienkos, "Politics. . ." See also Angela Pienkos, *A Brief History of Federation Life Insurance of America, 1913-1976* (Milwaukee: Haertlein Graphics, 1976); Still, pp. 272-73.

fire departments. In these years, the traditionally important political role played by the clergy and the press waned. Although Polonia's organizational vitality was apparent during this era (indeed, one of the Polish community's most vital cultural groups, the Polish Women's Cultural Club, "Polanki," was formed as recently as 1953), at the same time new generations of American Poles were moving -- physically as well as spiritually — out of Polonia in large numbers. And, in the case of Milwaukee, as opposed to Chicago, Detroit and New Jersey, relatively few new immigrants from Poland, certainly no more than 10,000 persons, settled in the community after World War II. Lacking an infusion of "new blood," the vitality of Polonia could only be adversely affected.

The most recent "stage" has witnessed the decline of the old Polonia organizational and institutional activity. Several traditionally Polish parishes have already lost their distinctly ethnic character as neighborhoods in which they are located have changed. Many Polonia secular organizations have ceased to exist except on paper, and those which remain have in most cases experienced steady declines in membership with persons over the age of sixty the predominant activists. Even among these groups, foreign-born Poles tend to be found in far higher proportions than their share of the entire Polonia would lead one to expect. In Milwaukee at least, Polish ethnic involvement is strongly associated with foreign birth, the maintaining of close ties with families and friends still in Poland, and knowledge of the Polish language. Proportionately few American-born Poles take part in organized Polonia affairs.[11]

On the other hand, every contemporary Polish American politician is either a second, third or fourth generation descendant of Polish immigrants. In winning office, most of these men have clearly benefitted from voter identification with their ethnic surnames. But few appear to perceive their own success as a measure of recognition for the Polish Americans of Milwaukee. Nor do they see themselves as responsible to Polonia's organizations as such, although those who belong to a Polish American group often present informal reports to fellow members when they attend their meetings. None appear to think that they owe their elections to

---

[11]According to membership statistics of the Polanki Women's club between 1953 and 1973, foreign-born women made up a significant portion of the total throughout the twenty year period, and between 1953 and 1966 they made up over 60% in all. Angela Pienkos, *Polanki: The Polish Women's Cultural Club of Milwaukee* (Milwaukee: The Franklin Press, 1973), p. 23. See also Donald Pienkos, "Ethnic Orientations among Polish Americans," *International Migration Review*, 11, (1977), 350-362.

support from organized Polonia groups. However, since some influential business and civic leaders continue to belong to Polonia organizations, politicians do look to these individuals for financial assistance in their campaigns.

One group is widely recognized as the most prominent association of Polish American business and professional men, lawyers and politicians in the Milwaukee metropolitan area. This organization, the Milwaukee Society of the Polish National Alliance fraternal insurance society was formed in 1921 and in 1976 numbered over three-hundred male members. Its membership roster listed seventeen public office holders in 1976, including US Congressman Zablocki, two county judges, one of the city's two Polish Americans in the state senate and four of the six Polish Americans representing Milwaukee districts in the state assembly. Seven Polish Americans in county government and eight men who were once politically active but who had since retired from public service were also listed as Society members as were a number of city and county administrative and supervisory personnel of Polish descent. The Milwaukee Society's monthly meetings, together with a variety of social activities that it sponsors (golf outings, baseball and football games, bowling, and a "Polish American of the Year" banquet, etc.) allow politically ambitious Polish Americans some excellent opportunities to meet prominent businessmen belonging to the organization. Evidence of the Milwaukee Society's continuing influence is in the success of its "political affairs committee," which pressured the governor of the state to appoint one of its members to fill a vacancy on the circuit court in July, 1978.[12]

For Polish American politicians in Milwaukee, Polish ethnic interests continue to be defined in terms of the traditional politics of local recognition. Importance is placed on arranging government proclamations to commemorate the birthdates of patriotic figures like Kosciuszko and Pulaski and the anniversaries of historic events such as the Constitution of May 3, 1791. Recognition politics also includes the nomination and appointment of worthy Polish Americans to local judgeships and regulatory commissions. One significant exception is the recent effort by the Polish American legislative contingent in conjunction with the Polish American Congress to win state funding for Polish studies courses at the

---

[12] *Milwaukee Sentinel,* December 17, 1977; *Milwaukee Journal,* July 12, 1978, p. 1.

University of Wisconsin in Milwaukee. In March, 1978, the legislature authorized adding over $59,000 to the university budget to hire faculty members in the fields of Polish history, language and literature.[13]

Noteworthy in the political history of Milwaukee's Polonia has been the existence of internal discord in a community where solidarity has often been a goal rather than a reality. Several examples of internal political conflict can be briefly described here. Already mentioned, of course, was the rising popularity of the socialist movement among Milwaukee Polish workers, a phenomenon which met with the most vitriolic of reactions from the Catholic Church between 1900 and the 1930's. Equally divisive was Polish criticism of the Church for its failure to elevate any Polish priests of stature to the rank of bishop.[14] A lengthy series of harsh attacks on Church policy published in Michael Kruszka's *Kuryer Polski* led the archbishop of the Milwaukee diocese in 1912 to forbid Polish Catholics to read the paper under the threat of excommunication. Though a Pole, Edward Kozlowski, was appointed an auxiliary bishop of Milwaukee in 1914, the bitterness generated by the controversy was not quickly healed.

In 1946, another fissure inside Polonia was exposed. The three-term US Congressman from Milwaukee's heavily Polish Fourth District, Thaddeus Wasielewski, was upset in the Democratic party primary. The winner in a bitter contest was a 27 year old unionist with pronounced leftist sympathies named Edmund Bobrowicz. Heavily backed by the CIO and Leo Krzycki's old South Side socialist forces, Bobrowicz proved a formidable rival against the conservative incumbent, an attorney whose own campaign suffered from ineffective management. Wasielewski had also alienated organized labor by his opposition to unemployment compensation legislation. Moreover, poor economic conditions made 1946 a Republican year around the country and the GOP capitalized on inflation, housing shortages and labor unrest to win control of Congress for the first time since 1930. Polonia was disenchanted with the Democrats for yet another reason. Many Poles viewed the Teheran, Yalta and Potsdam meetings as signalling American recognition of Soviet domination over postwar Poland. In

---

[13] *Milwaukee Journal*, December 18, 19, 1977; July 19, 1978.
[14] Anthony Kuzniewski, "Milwaukee's Poles, 1866-1918: The Rise and Fall of a Model Community," *Milwaukee History* (Spring, 1978), 13-24. The broader subject of Church-Polish relations during the years before 1914 is discussed by Victor Greene, *For God and Country* (Madison: The State Historical Society, 1975).

Milwaukee, they deserted their Polish Democratic Congressman in favor of Polish candidates running in the Republican primary, thus losing Wasielewski thousands of needed votes.

After his narrow defeat, Wasielewski continued the fight against Bobrowicz by campaigning as an independent in the general election. His action certainly deprived Bobrowicz of victory; it also damaged his standing with party regulars as the traditionally Democratic seat fell to the GOP. In 1948, Democratic state Senator Clement Zablocki was presented with a golden opportunity to win back the seat, which he has held to this date.[15]

Table 4. 1946 and 1948 Congressional Election Returns from the Fourth District

1946 Election Results		1948 Election Results	
Primary Election	**Vote**	**Primary Election**	**Vote**
E. Bobrowicz (D)	11,998	C. Zablocki (D)	26,317
T. Wasielewski (D)	10,713		
Total Republican Primary Vote	40,713	Total Republican Primary Vote	39,231
Republican Primary Vote Cast for Three Polish Candidates	(9,710)	(No Poles participated in the Republican Primary)	
General Election		**General Election**	
E. Bobrowicz (D)	44,398	C. Zablocki (D)	89,391
J. Brophy (R)	49,144	J. Brophy (R)*	63,161
T. Wasielewski (Independent)*	38,502	E. Bobrowicz (Peoples)	5,051

*Denotes incumbent

Understandably, the relatively few successful efforts to rally the Polish population have centered upon appeals to patriotic and religious sentiments. For example, American involvement in World War I was immensely popular since President Wilson's public endorsement of Polish independence was one of the reasons for US entry into that conflict. During and immediately after World War II, the Polish relief effort in Milwaukee raised over $170,000 in behalf of homeless and displaced countrymen in Europe. More recently, the 1966 "Millenium" observances recalling Poland's thousand years of nationhood and Christianity, and the 1973 celebrations honoring the five hundredth anniversary of the birth of

---

[15]Borun and Jakusz-Gostomski, p. 290; Lawrence Eklund, "CIO's 'Jimmy Higgins' Defeated Wasielewski," *Milwaukee Journal*, August 12, 1946, p. 12. Krzycki headed the pro-Soviet American Slav Congress during the World War. See D. Pienkos, "Politics. . .," 192 n. Wasielewski did not seek the Congressional nomination in 1948, but did challenge Zablocki in the 1950 Democratic primary. Zablocki won handily, receiving 72% of the vote.

the astronomer Kopernik (latinized to Copernicus) have been highly successful efforts to rally Polonia.[16]

In sum, the Polish Americans, while comprising Milwaukee's second largest white ethnic group for more than eighty years, have been effectively limited in the role they have played in city politics. This has primarily been due to the pre-eminence of the Germans and the Irish. While the Germans too have been sharply divided on both religious and political grounds, their far superior numbers, as well as higher socio-economic status have enabled them to dominate the city politically. And, while fewer in numbers within the population, Irish Americans have long played a key role in both city and county politics. Indeed, their prominence in county affairs is legendary. In 1977, for example, an Irishman held the chief administrative position in Milwaukee County, that of county executive, having just won election to succeed another Irishman who had held the office since its creation in 1960. At least 16 of 33 county judges were Irish and three of the six countywide elective offices were also held by individuals of Irish descent.[17] Given these facts, Polonia's politicians, while hardly unambitious themselves, have had to be content to play secondary roles in local affairs. Since the "Polish vote" has never amounted to more than one-fifth of the city electorate, Polonia leaders have placed greatest emphasis upon delivering a bloc vote in favor of candidates who promise the most to the Polish community as the sure method of winning political influence.

The Political Record: A Review

As far back as 1892 we in Milwaukee had Poles in every level of public service, from policemen to state senator... Nowhere in any other Polish settlement in all America did Poles so frequently achieve so many high offices as in Milwaukee, not in Buffalo, nor Detroit, not even Chicago where the largest number of Poles lived.

Wenceslaus Kruszka, 1906.

---

[16]For example, see Francis Swietlik, Chairman, Komitet Ratunkowy Polonii w Milwaukee, *Wisconsin American Relief for Poland* (Milwaukee: Nowiny Press, 1946); Clement Zablocki, Chairman, The Poland Millenium Committee, *Wisconsin's Observance of the Polish Millenium* (Milwaukee, 1966); Edward Tomasik, Chairman, Wisconsin Kopernik Committee, *1973 Kopernik Quincentennial Observance* (Cudahy, Wisconsin, 1973); Angela Pienkos, *Polanki,* and the 1946 volume under the general editorship of Borun and Jakusz-Gostomski, a significant demonstration in itself of community cooperation.

[17]Still, pp. 258-67; Sally Miller, "Milwaukee Retrospective: A Profile of Reform," a paper delivered at the University of Wisconsin-Milwaukee, April 3, 1974. On the political talents of the Irish, see Andrew Greeley, *That Most Distressful Nation: The Taming of the American Irish* (Chicago: Quadrangle Books, 1972), pp. 204-207. Greeley places the predilection for politics along with the Catholic Church and problems with alcohol as the three elements passed on in the Irish cultural heritage (p. 8).

Few Polish surnames are found in the membership rosters of the socially prestigious clubs or in the ranks of the top corporate management personnel of the area . . . (This) is in sharp contrast to their prominence in the political sphere.

>
> Henry Schmandt, Donald Vogel, and John Goldbach, *Milwaukee: A Contemporary Profile* (1971.[18]

These two observations, made nearly seventy years apart from one another, accurately characterize the Polish Americans' political experience in Milwaukee. Low on the socio-economic and status ladder, they regarded political achievement as a major compensation from the outset.

The first Pole to win local office was an immigrant tavernkeeper named August Rudzinski who was elected to a seat on the Milwaukee County Board of Supervisors in 1878. From this date forward, Polish American office holders were nearly always to be found as members of the county board, as aldermen belonging to the city's common council and as state legislators. The first Polish alderman, August Rudzinski's son Theodore, was elected in April, 1882, and later the same year Francis Borchardt became the first assemblyman dispatched to the state capital in Madison from the South Side's fourteenth ward. In 1892, Michael Kruszka was elected to the state senate, becoming the first Pole anywhere in the country to gain this post.

As the Polish American electorate grew in numbers, an increasingly large contingent of Poles won local offices. After 1908, at least one served as a Milwaukee ward alderman in every session of the city's common council. Between 1908 and 1940, twenty-six men of Polish origin were elected to the twenty-five member council for an average of between three and four per session. The peak years of Polish American aldermanic representation came between 1940 and 1964. For most of this period, the council included twenty-seven members, five of whom were Polish, and between 1948 and 1956, six Polish Americans were on the council. In addition, between 1918 and 1964 at least one, and sometimes two, Polish American aldermen representing the small North Side Polonia complemented the larger Polish contingent from the South Side wards.

---

[18]Kruszka, part 3, p. 133; Henry Schmandt, John Goldbach and Donald Vogel, *Milwaukee: A Contemporary Profile* (New York: Praeger Publishers, 1971), p. 12. Still strongly supports the views of Kruszka about the Poles' political ambitions throughout the sections of his history treating local politics.

Since 1954, the size of the common council has been reduced three times through reapportionment. With the enlargemesnt of the populations living in each remaining ward there has been a consequent decline in the strength of Polish American aldermanic representation, already weakened by Polish outmigration into the suburbs. In the 1972 and 1976 aldermanic elections, only one of the sixteen council members was Polish, though five city wards retain a sizeable Polish American population.

Polish Americans on the County Board of Supervisors, elected from both the city of Milwaukee and the surrounding suburban districts, became permanent fixtures from the beginning of the century. During most of this period at least three Poles have served on the county board. The 1976 elections saw four Poles and one individual who is half-Polish winning office. For the first time in many years, a politician from the small North Side Polonia was also elected a supervisor in 1972.

Polish Americans have been consistently successful in winning election to the state senate and assembly. At least one has been in the assembly without interruption since 1932, and fewer than three Poles were elected in only one year, 1938. In three election years (1954, 1956, 1958) five Poles won, while in eight others (1940, 1944, 1950, 1952, 1960, 1964, 1968, 1970), four were victorious. In 1972, 1974 and 1976, six of the twenty-four assemblymen in the Milwaukee delegation to the ninety-nine member assembly were Polish.

After Kruszka completed his state senate term in 1896, the next Pole elected to that body was a Republican attorney, John Kleczka, who served between 1908 and 1912. From 1918, at least one Pole served in the thirty-three member state senate in each of its sessions, and between 1930 and 1978, two of Milwaukee county's nine member delegation were Poles.

A decade-by-decade review of Polish American participation in local elective bodies shows remarkable consistency in their level of success; indeed, since 1920 the proportion of Poles elected Milwaukee aldermen, county board supervisors and state legislators appears to have fairly accurately reflected their numbers within the total population in the county.

Several Polish Americans have won major elective offices in Milwaukee. Since 1918, three Poles have been Congressmen from the South Side's Fourth District. The first to sit in Congress was a Republican, John Kleczka, who also happened to be the first Polish American ever elected to the House of Representatives. Kleczka

Table 5. Polish Americans Holding Elective Political Office in Milwaukee County for Selected Years Between 1910 and 1976

Number of Positions in the following Governmental Bodies, with number of Polish Elected Officials in Parentheses

Year	City Council	County Board	State Senate	State Assembly	Total Number of Elected Officials	Pct. Polish
1910	25 (2)	20 (2)	6 (1)	20 (1)	71	8.5%
1920	25 (2)	20 (3)	6 (1)	20 (2)	71	11.3
1930	25 (4)	20 (3)	6 (2)	20 (1)	71	14.1
1940	27 (5)	20 (3)	6 (2)	20 (4)	73	19.2
1950	27 (6)	20 (3)	7 (2)	20 (4)	74	20.3
1960	20 (5)	24 (2)	9 (2)	24 (4)	77	16.9
1970	19 (3)	25 (3)	9 (2)	24 (4)	77	15.6
1976	16 (1)	25 (5)	9 (2)	24 (6)	74	18.9

served two terms between 1919 and 1923. He was followed from 1941 to 1947 by a Democrat, Thaddeus Wasielewski. Since 1948, another Democrat, Clement Zablocki, has won sixteen consecutive terms in the House of Representatives, the most for any Pole in the country's history. In 1977, Zablocki was elected chairman of the Committee on International Relations, the highest legislative responsibility achieved by a Pole in the US.

Historically, Polish Democrats were frequently successful in winning city-wide elections for comptroller, the chief financial officer in Milwaukee. In 1890, Roman Czerwinski won the first of two consecutive two-year terms when he was elected on a ticket along with Mayor George Peck. Thereafter, the practice of nominating worthy Poles for the post of "Polish mayor" (as many Poles proudly if pragmatically termed the comptroller's position) became a common one: Peter Pawinski held the office between 1902 and 1906; August Gawin served a term from 1908 to 1910; and Louis Kotecki was elected to eight consecutive terms between 1912 and 1933. Since 1933, however, only one Polish American, John Kalupa, has been comptroller, although several others, notably Zablocki, were unsuccessful in their efforts to become "Polish mayors" during this period.[19]

---

[19] Held responsible for the questionable financial actions he had unwittingly approved, Kotecki went berserk, wounded his deputy and then took his own life. *Milwaukee Journal*, July 11, 12, 1933. See also Jerome Watrous, ed., *Memoirs of Milwaukee County* (Madison: Western Historical Association, 1909), Volume II, for an early biography.

Of all the Polish Americans who were active in Milwaukee politics, Kotecki as a citywide elected official seems to have possessed the best opportunity to have risen to still higher office. Yet he never challenged Daniel Hoan for the mayoral nomination, even though the socialist incumbent was often critical of Kotecki's policies and supported opposition candidates for comptroller in every election.

Beginning in the 1950's, Polish Americans were increasingly frequent victors in countywide elections for sheriff, treasurer, coroner and register of deeds. Elections to these positions were similar to those of the state legislature in that they were partisan affairs. It is thus likely that candidates with Polish surnames running as Democrats have had great advantages in such elections. Indeed, the possession of a well-known and readily identifiable Polish surname has helped many a career in local politics. A popular South Sider named Joseph Michalski sat on the County Board for nearly three decades up to his death in 1945. Clemens Michalski, no relation, served in a variety of local offices without interruption from 1934 until his retirement in 1968, first as state assemblyman, then as city alderman, county sheriff, and county clerk. Yet another Michalski, Edward, again no relation, presently is a member of the Milwaukee School Board. Other examples are numerous: a prominent South Side attorney named Richard B. Nowakowski began a political career extending from the early 1950's through the late 1970's as a state assemblyman, alderman and most recently as an appointed member of the City Harbor Commission. Richard C. Nowakowski, no relation, rose to the chairmanship of the County Board of Supervisors in 1972, the first Pole to attain this post, after serving in the state legislature and the county board. Other notable Polish surnames in Milwaukee political history have included Zablocki, Barczak and Kleczka. (Particularly well-known non-Polish surnames in state and local politics have included La Follette, Zimmerman, Smith and Zeidler, among others.)

However, the Poles' success in local politics has had its limits too. Only one Pole, Leonard Fons, was a serious mayoral candidate, and he was badly trounced in his 1952 campaign at the hands of the socialist incumbent, Frank Zeidler. Fons won only 28 percent of the total vote in capturing one of the twenty-seven wards, the heavily Polish 14th aldermanic district.[20]

In 1957, two Polish Congressmen, Zablocki and Republican Alvin O'Konski took part in a special primary election to determine the successor to the US Senate seat that had become vacant with the death of Joseph McCarthy. The presence of a Polish candidate in each party primary probably spelled defeat for both men, although

---

[20]Sarah Ettenheim, *How Milwaukee Voted* (Milwaukee: Institute of Governmental Affairs, 1970), p. 128.

it is doubtful whether either could have won the general election which followed.[21]

Table 6. Results of the Special US Senate Primary Election, July 30, 1957.

Republican Senatorial Candidates		Democratic Senatorial Candidates	
William Kohler	109,256	William Proxmire	86,341
Glen Davis	100,532	Clement Zablocki	56,817
Alvin O'Konski	66,784		
Warren Knowles	23,996		
Minor Candidates	16,720		

Proximire upset Kohler in the general election, August 27, 1957, 435,985 to 312,931 with 23,573 for minor candidates.

In the 1966 Wisconsin primary, a Milwaukee state senator, Richard Zaborski, was defeated by the narrowest of margins in a bid for the Democratic party nomination for the office of treasurer. Zaborski received 100,466 votes, while his chief opponent in a three-cornered race won with 101,249 (only to be handily defeated in the general election by the Republican incumbent).[22] Most recently, in 1976, two Poles campaigned in the nonpartisan primary election for the office of Milwaukee County executive. In a five way contest, they ran poorly and finished third and fourth. Neither was thus able to gain entry into the general election that followed.[23]

Least success has been enjoyed by Poles in winning judicial offices and only six out of over two hundred individuals who have been judges in Milwaukee County since 1900 have been Polish. In 1978, two Poles, Robert Miech and Michael Skwierawski, were in office, out of a total of thirty-six judges with Milwaukee County jurisdictions.[24]

---

[21] *The Wisconsin Blue Book, 1958* (Madison: Wisconsin Legislative Reference Library, 1958), pp. 66-67.

Clement Zablocki, born in Milwaukee in 1912, was originally a school teacher and a church organist. Closely associated through family ties with many Polonia groups on Milwaukee's South Side, Zablocki has been the quintessential ethnic politician throughout his career, ever solicitous of his Polish American constituency. At the same time, he has become a serious student of international politics in the House of Representatives. Politically, Zablocki has been cautiously ambitious, first winning election to the Wisconsin State Senate at the age of thirty in 1942. After an unsuccessful effort to become "Polish mayor" in 1948 he was elected to Congress to fill the seat once held by Kleczka and Wasielewski. His last attempt to seek higher office was in 1957 when he lost the Democratic primary election for US Senator. When Frank Zeidler decided not to seek a fourth mayoral term in 1960, Zablocki chose not to contest a primary which would have pitted him against another Milwaukee Congressman, Henry Reuss (who had in 1957 stepped aside to allow Zablocki to be "Milwaukee's candidate" for the Senate) and the eventual victor, State Senator Henry Maier.

[22] *The Wisconsin Blue Book, 1968* (Madison: Wisconsin Legislative Reference Library, 1968), p. 705.

[23] Milwaukee County Clerk Thomas Zablocki received 18,364 votes (12.3 percent) and state Assemblyman Joseph Czerwinski 10,672 votes (7.2 percent) in the primary election. Neither carried a single ward or suburb in the balloting. Even in the five heavily Polish wards of Milwaukee, Zablocki, holder of the same surname as that of the popular US Congressman (though no relation), won only 13.9 percent of the vote. In these wards, Czerwinski received a 12.4 percent share—his best showing in the primary. *Milwaukee Journal*, February 18, 1976, p. 22.

[24] The others were John Kleczka and Francis Swietlik, judges of the Circuit Court, Michael Blenski and Thaddeus Pruss, both of the County Civil Court, and Francis Gregorski of the Municipal Traffic Court.

Why were Milwaukee's Polish Americans historically successful in local politics, even as early as the end of the nineteenth century? What accounts for the continuing presence of a large contingent of Polish elected officials in Milwaukee? Finally, how does their success in certain political areas square with the fact of their near absence from citywide elective office and the judiciary?

In trying to answer these kinds of questions, some observers of ethnic groups have focused their attention upon the character of the ethnic community itself. For example, they cite the research conducted by the political scientist, Robert Dahl, in New Haven, the work of a sociologist of the Polish ethnic group in America, Helena Lopata, and even popular opinion on these questions. Though different from one another in many respects, all share the view that an ethnic group's political fate is best explained in terms of the community's own characteristics. According to Dahl, for one, ethnic voting behavior is but a function of the ethnic population's working class homogeneity. As a growing proportion of the ethnic population rises to middle class status, its members become increasingly heterogeneous in their political thinking as well. Inevitably, voting for a candidate on the basis of shared ethnicity loses its appeal since no class consensus over policy issues remains. With the ethnic community gradually becoming assimilated into the larger community, ethnic politics must be seen, according to Dahl, as "clearly a transitional phenomenon."[25] In applying this thesis to the Milwaukee Polish American experience, one might have expected that the heavily working class Polish electorate of the period prior to World War II would have solidified behind Polish political leaders espousing their cause, and that a noticeable decline in the number of successful Polish politicans would have been registered over the past three decades. In fact, the actual experience of the Poles has run counter to both expectations.

A second thesis, offered by Lopata, argues that Polonia's "institutional completeness" determines the level of Polish activity (and presumably success) in local politics. The more "institutionally complete" the ethnic community—in its ability to satisfy the Poles' religious, educational, social, recreational and informational needs—the less likely they would be to take an active role in the politics of the larger community of which Polonia was a part.[26] Yet,

---

[25]Robert Dahl, *Who Governs? Democracy and Power in an American City* (New Haven: Yale University Press, 1961), pp. 34-36.
[26]Helena Lopata, *Polish Americans: Status Competition in an Ethnic Community* (Englewood Cliffs, N. J.: Prentice-Hall, 1976), pp. 66-67.

Poles were involved in local Milwaukee politics as early as the 1880's, a time in which the institutional life of Polonia was far more "complete" and vital than it is today. Conversely, the decline of Polonia activity in recent years has not been accompanied by any extraordinary political achievements of Poles seeking local office.

A third view expressed by Poles in Milwaukee and elsewhere has focused upon the lack of Polish ethnic solidarity as the reason for Polonia's failure to gain certain high offices. This idea assumes that a large community of otherwise diverse individuals can unite on the basis of one shared trait, their ethnicity, to become a cohesive political force.[27] It is a highly doubtful assertion.

To understand the Polish Americans' political experience, we must go beyond analyses of Polonia itself and direct attention to some of the salient features of the Milwaukee political environment in which the Poles found themselves. The pre-eminence of the Germans and Irish in community affairs, a factor which inevitably limited the Polish Americans' opportunities to play a leading role in city politics, has been noted. Three other historically important factors were: (1) the existence of sharp inter-party competition in Milwaukee during the last two decades of the nineteenth and first thirty years of the twentieth centuries; (2) the availability of a large number of local elective offices open to enterprising Polish candidates in both the city and the county; and (3) the character of the electoral system.

Party Competition: From the 1880's and into the 1930's, Milwaukee municipal politics was shaped by an enduring inter-party rivalry for control of local government. Until 1910, the Democrats and Republicans were usually the main contestants; afterward, local elections generally pitted the social democratic forces against the "fusionists," as the Democrats and Republicans were originally termed when they banded together to battle the Socialist party led by Victor Berger, Emil Seidel and Daniel Hoan.[28] Though municipal and county elections after 1912 were turned into non-partisan affairs by state law, most contests for these offices continued to be recognized by the voters as elections pitting

---

[27]Edward Kantowicz, *Polish-American Politics in Chicago, 1888-1940* (Chicago and London: University of Chicago Press, 1975), pp. 217-18; and included in the following chapter. Eklund.

[28]Still, pp. 279-320; 356-95; Miller. The overwhelming Polish vote in favor of populist candidates in the 1886 elections helped that party sweep the county races and elect a U S Congressman. This followed the repression of a Polish workmen's strike at the Bay View rolling mills by units of the Wisconsin National Guard. The strike was part of a citywide action led by the Knights of Labor in favor of the eight hour work day. Jerry Cooper, "The Wisconsin National Guard in the Milwaukee Riots of 1886," *Wisconsin Magazine of History,* 55, (1971).

socialists against anti-socialist candidates. Since the mass migration of Poles to Milwaukee coincided with this era of political competition, "winning the Polish vote" was perceived by local politicians as having a critical bearing upon the outcomes of many elections. Even when the actual number of Polish voters was relatively small, Poles were courted with nominations to important elective offices and promises of political appointments. Thus, from 1890 to 1933, Poles served as city comptrollers for a total of thirty-one years, often after having defeated Polish opponents. While the Poles in the main supported Democratic candidates locally, a sizeable number voted, between 1910 and the late 1930's, for socialists and La Follette's progressive Republicans. Michael Kruszka's influential *Kuryer Polski* maintained a progressive editorial orientation from 1900 until 1938, and several unsuccessful tries at establishing a Polish language socialist paper were made before 1920. One of the city's leading Republican politicians was Congressman John Kleczka, and one of its most prominent labor leaders was the socialist, Leo Krzycki. Indicative, perhaps, of the political divisions within Polonia is the fact that between 1918 and 1932, five of the twelve Poles who were elected to the state assembly from Milwaukee were socialists, four others were Republicans and three were Democrats. A Polish socialist, Walter Polakowski, held a heavily Polish South Side state senate seat from 1922 to 1934, and three of the other four Poles to be elected to the state senate between 1908 and 1934 were Republicans.[29] The election of Franklin Roosevelt and the coming of the New Deal brought new life to the local Democratic party, however, and by the late 1930's, it had become dominant in both the city and the county. This development coincided with the demise of both the Socialist party in Milwaukee and Philip La Follette's Wisconsin Progressive party, which had broken away from the Republicans in 1934. In fact, the end of inter-party competition in local elections had important consequences for the Poles: though their actual share of the electorate rose, the Polish vote itself ceased to be as crucial a factor in deciding citywide elections. Indeed, the number of Polish candidates for citywide office declined sharply after 1933.[30]

---

[29] Brief biographical information about a number of Milwaukee Polish progressives and socialists is in Donald Pienkos, "Politics. . .," 190-201.

[30] Even John Kalupa (1899-1975), the last Polish city comptroller, was hardly secure, despite a tenure of fourteen years in the position. In 1972, he refused to step down from the post and was overwhelmed by a candidate sponsored by the mayor. Receiving only 56,000 votes to the victor's 133,000, Kalupa lost all sixteen wards of the city, including his own heavily Polish fourteenth ward. Thaddeus Stawicki, Executive Secretary, *Board of Election Commissioners, City of Milwaukee: 32nd Biennial Report* (Milwaukee, 1973), p. 53.

The Availability of Office: The continued presence of large numbers of Milwaukee Polish aldermen, county supervisors and state legislators is a phenomenon not simply explained in terms of the size of the Polish population itself. After all, Detroit, with an even larger Polish American population, has traditionally possessed fewer Polish representatives in local government than Milwaukee. More important is the fact that numerically large legislative assemblies whose members represent relatively small constituencies have been characteristic of Milwaukee and Wisconsin. For example, the Polish American population greatly benefitted from the fact that the city was carved into as many as 27 aldermanic districts, each including (in 1931) only about 22,000 residents. In the same year, each of Chicago's fifty city wards included approximately 65,000 persons. Legislative assembly districts and county board constituencies have in similar fashion been small, and more legislative districts including large Polish populations have been found in Milwaukee than in Chicago, Buffalo, and Detroit. Since Milwaukee's Polish American population spilled over into several district units, Poles were able to play a significant role in the politics of a fairly large number of constituencies.[31] Had the city and county been apportioned differently, for example, into fewer and larger units, or had elections been held on an at-large basis, it is doubtful that Poles would have done as well. Since 1972, the common council has been reduced in size to sixteen members, with each ward including about 41,000 residents. Since this reapportionment, only one Pole has served in each session of the council, although five city wards still possess sizable Polish populations. The experience of the fifteen member Milwaukee School Board is also worth noting. Elected on an at-large basis, the board has only rarely possessed even one elected Polish member within its ranks.

Some Consequences of Political Reform: The 1912 state law designed to weaken the influence of the Milwaukee socialists required that municipal elections in Milwaukee be nonpartisan. Even before that action, civil service reforms affecting the hiring

---

[31] A check of available data regarding the legislative constituencies for those states having significant Polish populations is particularly instructive. In 1976, the average state senate district in Wisconsin included 133,877 inhabitants, compared with 188,372 for the average Illinois state senate district, 233,753 for Michigan, 235,949 for Pennsylvania, 304,021 for New York, and 322,788 for Ohio. The average Wisconsin assembly district had 44,626 residents, to 62,791 for Illinois, 58,115 for Pennsylvania, 80,751 for Michigan, 107,596 for Ohio, and 121,608 for New York. Paul Albright, *et. al., The Book of the States* (Lexington, Ky.: The Council of State Governments, 1976), Volume XXI, pp. 42-43. Moreover, while generalizations about the differential effects of legislative apportionment in varying state environments are dangerous, it is true that Wisconsin had achieved a more equitable legislative reapportionment as early as 1950. For developments in Wisconsin, Illinois, Michigan and New York, see Wilder Crane and Meredith Watts, *State Legislative Systems* (Englewood Cliffs, N. J.: Prentice-Hall, 1968), pp. 24-34.

and tenure of city employees had limited the power of political officials to dispense government jobs as rewards to their campaign supporters. The coming to power of "clean government" socialist rule under Emil Seidel (Mayor from 1910 to 1912) and Dan Hoan (Mayor from 1916 to 1940) brought an effective end to the era of political patronage and influence peddling in city politics that had characterized the administration of Mayor David Rose (1898-1906, 1908-1910).[32] For the Poles, all these developments had an important political impact in hurrying the disappearance of the old party organizations in Milwaukee which had traditionally dominated the selection of nominees for elective office and heavily influenced the outcome of municipal elections. As the role played by the old "machines" diminished, the importance of incumbency in high office was enhanced. With effective competition for office limited to the Democratic primary and nonpartisan elections where turnout was generally light and voter recognition of the incumbent's name and record provided a great advantage over lesser known challengers, Polish and non-Polish politicians in Milwaukee became increasingly cautious in challenging incumbents for higher office. Usually, contests have taken place only in those situations where vacancies exist. For example, Clement Zablocki won his congressional seat in the heavily Polish Fourth District in 1948 against a non-Pole *when* the previous Polish incumbent, Wasielewski had decided not to run. Only when Zablocki's state senate seat became available with his decision to run for Congress did a Polish assemblyman, Casimir Kendziorski, announce his decision to seek the senate seat. When Kendziorski retired in 1974, two Polish assemblymen, Gerald Kleczka and Raymond Tobiasz campaigned to succeed him in an election won by Kleczka.

Electoral reform also had other effects. Though Poles were still able to dominate elections occurring in those wards where large numbers of their countrymen were concentrated, the end of machine politics sharply reduced their chances of mounting serious campaigns for citywide office. The Polish American community already lacked the other resources, financial and leadership, vital to playing a significant role in local politics, and the end of organized political party competition meant that the only remaining means of gaining influence, their vote strength, could no longer be translated into a certain share of the nominations to high office. There was an

---

[32]Sarah Ettenheim, "Group Endorsement in Milwaukee Non-Partisan Elections," University of Wisconsin-Milwaukee M.A. Thesis, 1963, pp. 2ff; Still, pp. 306 ff.

added problem since, in Milwaukee, a candidate's ability to win at the ward level is largely dependent on his success in mobilizing grass roots support over issues of neighborhood, rather than citywide concern. Hence, at least for the Poles, the holding of aldermanic or supervisory office has not proven to be a stepping stone to higher elective positions.[33]

Second, relatively few Poles have been able to win appointment to any of the various city and county commissions which are responsible for policy-making in local government. While such appointments pay only nominal salaries, they nonetheless are prestigious and have been much sought after by politically active citizens. In 1956, out of 40 city commissions with 407 members, sixteen had major policy-making responsibilities and included 117 members. At that time, 28 Poles were appointed members of all commissions, with 10 sitting on the "major" commissions. In 1976, 350 persons on 42 commissions included 27 Poles, of whom 13 belonged to the 16 more important policy-making bodies. Poles had a somewhat better record of winning appointment to policy-making commissions at the county level. In 1976, there were 16 county commissions with 140 members, 18 of whom were Polish. Of the six major commissions operating at the county level, eleven of the sixty-two members of these bodies were Polish.[34]

That relatively few Polish politicians have possessed the necessary qualifications to be seriously considered for higher office is indicated by the low number of Poles (in comparison with non-Poles) who have entered politics with professional careers behind them. A check of the occupations of 37 Poles elected to the state legislature between 1890 and 1942 found that only 32% had professional occupations at the time of their election, while 19% were small businessmen, 19% were skilled workers and 30% were

---

[33]Ettenheim, pp. 35ff., 46-47, 53ff.; Schmandt, *et. al.*

[34]Several Poles in 1976 held major commission responsibility, including Edmund Krawczyk, chairman of the five member County Civil Service Commission, Stanley Celichowski, chairman of the City Planning Commission, Casimir Koltunski, chairman of the City Board of Assessment, Richard B. Nowakowski, chairman of the City Harbor Commission, and Supervisor Emil Stanislawski, chairman of the County Commission on Aging. Both Celichowski and Nowakowski retired from their positions in 1977.

Municipal commissions with major policy-making responsibilities include: the Boards of Assessment, Estimates, Appeals, Review, Adult Education, and the School Board; as well as the commissions of City Planning, Civil Service, Public Debt, Police and Fire, Harbor, Housing, Capital Improvements (1956 only), Redevelopment Authority (1976 only), and Public Land (1956). Important county commissions include: Civil Service, Expressway and Transportation, Parks, Public Welfare, Community Relations, and Aging.

I am indebted to Professor Clarke Hagensick, Director of the UWM Institute of Governmental Affairs for helping me differentiate among these commissions, although I take full responsibility for the interpretation of the role played by Polish Americans on these bodies.

For a full listing of all city and county commissions, the manner in which their members are selected, their tenures in office and their salaries, see Schmandt, *et. al.,* Appendix.

manual laborers. Between 1950 and 1976, 22 Polish state legislators won office: of these, 32% were professionally employed, 18% were proprietors, 18% were skilled workmen and 32% were manual workers, practically the same as the earlier era. When these figures were compared with data gathered on the occupations of Wisconsin assemblymen in 1957 by Leon Epstein[35] and this author's check of the career backgrounds of Milwaukee legislators in selected years between 1950 and 1976, Polish legislators were found to be generally less likely to have possessed professional or business experience than non-Poles. In all, only six Poles were attorneys while they served in the legislature, three during each period. Perhaps even more important, Polish Americans in office continued to lag behind their non-Polish colleagues who were in office at the same time in terms of educational attainment.

In retrospect, then, the Poles of Milwaukee have played a secondary but salient role in local politics. While the major offices have eluded them, a host of Polish politicians have won elective offices at every level of local government. What of the future, however?

In the city itself, the day of the Poles seems over. The once tightly-knit organizational life of Polonia no longer exists, and many once powerful Polish institutions have either disappeared (e.g., the Polish press) or lost much of their ethnic character (a number of the parishes). As thousands of Poles have moved out of the city, new ethnic groups such as blacks and Spanish-speaking peoples have begun increasingly to make their presence felt.[36]

Table 7. The Relative Size of Selected Population Groups in Milwaukee, 1930-1970

	Total City Population	FOREIGN BORN AND FOREIGN STOCK POPULATIONS*						NON-WHITE AND MINORITY POPULATIONS	
		Germans	Pct.	Poles	Pct.	Blacks	Pct.	Native-American and Spanish	Pct.
1930	578,300	158,000	27.4	64,400	11.1	7,500	1.3	Negligible	.0
1950	637,400	99,120	15.6	47,000	7.4	22,130	3.5	2,000	0.3
1970	717,400	50,200	7.0	28,900	4.0	106,000	14.8	21,700	3.0

*These US census data, unfortunately, include only immigrants and individuals having at least one parent born in either Germany or Poland, and thus exclude later generations of persons of German or Polish heritage.

[35]Leon Epstein, *Politics in Wisconsin* (Madison: University of Wisconsin Press, 1958), pp. 192, 193.
[36]See Alice Ann Conner," Polish (Restaurant) Fare Hard to Find," *Milwaukee Journal*, September 20, 1977; and "Fons Leadership Ends at Savings and Loan," *Milwaukee Journal*, September 19, 1977, p. 14, for two recent reports documenting trends in Polonia. The deaths of two one-time Polonia political leaders within a few weeks of each other were also symbolic: note obituaries for Stanley Cybulski (October 6) and Clemens Michalski (October 21, 1977) in the *Milwaukee Journal*.

At the county, state and federal levels, however, Polish Americans seem likely to play important roles for some time to come. Individuals of Polish descent possessing the necessary qualifications and political contacts continue to win local office, although the dispersion of the Polish population throughout the county together with the impact of assimilation means that their success no longer depends primarily upon their appeal to Polish American voters.

EDWARD R. KANTOWICZ

The Limitations of Ethnic Politics: Polish Americans in Chicago*

The voting record of Polish Americans in Chicago can be summarized very briefly. They voted Democratic from the very beginning. In eighteen mayoral elections from 1889 to 1935, Chicago Poles gave a majority of their votes to the Democratic candidate in every instance. In thirteen presidential elections from 1888 to 1936, Polish voters delivered a Democratic majority in all but two cases.

More significant than the voting record, however, is the political strategy pursued by Polish American leaders. It was a strategy common to many emerging ethnic and racial groups in American society, a strategy of ethnic bloc voting, group pride, and a drive for greater recognition. The limitations of the strategy are important for an understanding not only of Poles in Chicago but of ethnic politics generally.

One can also ask a more specific question: why has there never been a Polish American mayor of Chicago? This question is often asked around the city in a tone of reproach to Chicago's largest ethnic group. Anton Cermak, representing a much smaller Czech community, fought his way to City Hall in 1931. Why hasn't Polonia in the years since then produced a Polish Cermak?

Polish American politicians have been generally of two types, respectables or bosses. But the history of Chicago politics indicates that the successful mayoral candidate has been a third type, a mixed politician. He has combined the boss' power drive and machine methods with a broker's skill in allying his machine with the respectable elements of the city. Mayor Carter Harrison II (1897-1905, 1911-1915) was a master of this sort of balancing act,

*From Edward R. Kantowicz, *Polish American Politics in Chicago,* 1888-1940 (Chicago and London: University of Chicago Press, 1975), pp. 208-19, 252-53. Reprinted with the permission of the author and the publisher.

combining his river ward allies with reform and independent voters. Though Bill Thompson (mayor, 1915-1923, 1927-1931) became almost a caricature of a corrupt boss, in his first race he gained support both from Protestant church leaders and from the lowest underworld elements in the city. And Tony Cermak, Chicago's most successful immigrant politico, also followed this same mixed-politics, broker model.

Cermak's life in Chicago was devoted singlemindedly to the capture of political power, in his own West Side Czech community and later in the city as a whole. Power-seeking was a fundamental trait in his personality, almost a disease inhabiting his body. In fact, this trait may have contributed to his death, for psychosomatic illness weakened his resistance to the assassin's bullet which felled him.[1] But before his tragic end, Cermak's power drive led him to the top in politics.

In seeking power, Cermak used the usual tools of the ward boss, firm ties with his own ethnic power base, control of patronage, and intimate knowledge of the party machinery. But he also developed exquisite skills as a political broker, essential skills in a heterogeneous city like Chicago, where power had to be forged out of many ethnic and economic groups. He first developed the broker's skill as director of the United Societies for Local Self Government, Chicago's leading antiprohibition lobby. In this post he led a coalition of often squabbling and jealous ethnic groups— the Irish, the Germans, and all the new immigrant groups—by focusing their attention on one goal, to keep Chicago wet.

In the 1920's, Cermak extended his broker's role and broadened his base by appealing to the conservative establishment and the thrifty middle class with a businesslike image as a master administrator of the county board.

When boss George E. Brennan died in 1928, Cermak used his skill as a broker to unite all the newer ethnic groups who were dissatisfied with Irish dominance of the Democratic party and thus to capture the Cook County party chairmanship. In the mayoral race in 1931, he successfully united many respectable businessmen and reformers with his ethnic, wet, working class support by a skillful use of his administrative record and a vigorous campaign against the discredited Thompson and his Republican

---

[1] Anton Cermak's biographer discusses in an appendix entitled "Leadership and Psychosomatic Analysis," the Chicago mayor's power drive and its role in his chronic suffering from colitis. He concludes that Cermak did not literally die of his gunshot wound but from complications brought on by colitis. Alex Gottfried, *Boss Cermak of Chicago* (Seattle: University of Washington Press, 1962), pp. 365-78.

administration. Cermak was fortunate in his opposition in 1931, for Big Bill's reputation was so unsavory that the immigrant boss found it relatively easy to look respectable.

Thus the essential elements in Cermak's rise to power were an unquenchable power drive, great skill at the delicate balancing act of broker politics, plus unusually good luck.[2]

An additional, subtle factor may have been involved as well. Cermak's ethnic group, the Czechs, was one of the smaller ones in Chicago. Among the new immigrant nationalities, it ranked roughly in the middle—less numerous than the Poles, Italians, or Jews, but more numerous than the Lithuanians, Greeks, or Yugoslavs.[3] As head of a relatively small ethnic group, he was under no illusions that he could succeed solely as a Czech leader; furthermore, other nationalities, which didn't want to replace Irish and WASP dominance with the tyranny of another large group, did not see the Czechs and their leader as a threat. His leadership of a marginal group assisted his performance as a broker.

Chicago, Polonia's capital, failed to produce a leader who combined a lust for power, skill at political brokering, and good luck, as Cermak did. No Polish American politician in Chicago successfully played this mixed role, halfway between boss and respectable.

The outstanding leaders of the first generation in Polonia's capital before World War I were John Smulski (1867-1928) and Stanley Kunz (1864-1946). Kunz, who attained some power and influence as a ward boss, had a distinctly unsavory reputation in the American press and could never have appealed successfully to the community as a whole. Kunz himself must have known this, for never in his long career did he seek an office outside his home district of "Polish Downtown," Chicago's oldest Polish settlement on the city's near North Side. On the other side, Smulski was eminently respectable, a banker, businessman, and attorney; but he was so respectable as to find politics distasteful, and thus he soon abandoned office-seeking. No other Polish leader of the first generation came any closer to combining the necessary ingredients than these two.

The same division between bosses and respectables persisted in the second generation (between the world wars). Polish politicians

---

[2]Ibid., p. 351.
[3]In 1930 the population figures for the new immigrant groups in Chicago (with percentage of total city population) were: Poles—401,316 (12%); Italians—181,861 (5%); Russians (Jews)—169,736 (5%); Czechs—122,089 (4%); Lithuanians—63,918 (2%); Yugoslavs—32,291 (1%); Greeks—26,384 (1%). Edward W. Burgess and Charles Newcomb, eds., *Census Data of the City of Chicago, 1930* (Chicago: University of Chicago Press, 1933), p. XV.

who became ward committeemen in the late twenties and thirties were generally local figures, powers in their own wards, but either unknown or lowly regarded in the city as a whole. When in 1929, Joe Przybylo, the thirty-first ward committeeman, ran for alderman against Frank Konkowski, a future committeeman, the Municipal Voters' League found the former "unfit for council service" and the latter "(despite) natural abilities and educational advantages, disqualified by low standards of public service." The man preferred by the MVL was Stanley Adamkiewicz, "preferred to opponents because of good intentions and willingness to take counsel with better citizens." Obviously none of these ward figures, neither those disapproved nor the one condescendingly tolerated, could have impressed the respectables in a wider contest.[4]

Perhaps the best, and certainly the most influential of the local ward figures, was Joseph Rostenkowski, or "Joe Rosty" as his friends called him. Son of a respected president of the Polish Roman Catholic Union fraternal association and nephew of a former Republican state legislator, Joe Rostenkowski served his political apprenticeship at the precinct level in the Kunz organization while earning a living in insurance and real estate. In 1930 he attained his first elective office, a seat in the state legislature, which he won in a revolt against Kunz's dominance of the district. In 1932 Joe Rosty became alderman of the thirty-second ward, the heart of Polish Downtown, and although he did not officially become ward committeeman until the late thirties, he soon established himself as the actual leader of the ward.

When Rostenkowski first ran for the legislature, the *Chicago Daily News* recommended him as a man who "bears a good reputation"; and throughout his career as ward boss, the Polish Downtown ward enjoyed a better press than it had during Kunz's heyday. But, though no major scandals erupted and no charges of corruption were levelled at Rosty, his career was, in most other ways, a classic example of a ward boss. During the hard Depression years, Rosty's ward organization kept busy distributing coal and food baskets and helping to pay gas and electric bills for constituents. He was a tireless worker for the Night of Stars gala, a Kelly-Nash fund-raising event held annually at the Chicago Amphitheatre. He attended carefully to the physical appearance of his ward, giving personal attention to garbage pickup and street cleaning, and taking a special interest in the construction of the Milwaukee Avenue subway from his position on the city council

[4]*Chicago Tribune*, February 19, 1929, p. 4.

transportation committee. And, most important, throughout the thirties and forties, his ward was one of the most productive of Democratic votes in the city.

Apparently the basis of his power at the local level was his personal relationship to his workers and to the voters. All who knew him, ally and political foe alike, emphasized his loyalty to friends and his faithfulness to his word. When the thirty-second ward organization brought foreign-born Poles to the federal building for their citizenship tests, it was not uncommon for one of the prospective citizens to answer the question, "Who is the president of the United States?" with the name of Joseph Rostenkowski.[5]

Joe Rostenkowski enjoyed more power and security in his own ward than he did recognition elsewhere in the city. He probably could have been slated for higher office if he had wanted to, for he was personally friendly with Mayor Edward Kelly, Cermak's successor. He was talked of as a possible successor to Frank Zintak as superior court clerk and also a potential candidate for sheriff. Kelly himself asked Rostenkowski to run for Congress in the early forties, but Rosty refused and put up Thomas Gordon instead. Unlike Anton Cermak or others who transcended a ward-boss background to reach higher office, Rosty was not a power-seeker, except in his own local milieu. Somewhat limited in intelligence and cunning, blunt, straightforward, and emotional, he was as strong as a feudal lord in Polish Downtown but was not the man to appeal to respectable America, any more than the other ward bosses of Polonia's capital were.

In the second generation, the respectables in politics tended to be lawyers and judges. Businessmen like Smulski, Smietanka, or Piotrowski of the first generation rarely went in for officeholding in these later years, since the Democratic machine had begun to centralize the slating process and there was little room for outsiders. Politicians who did not like the nitty-gritty of everyday politics usually played the game for a time in lower offices, but aimed for the relatively nonpolitical spots on the bench as soon as possible.

Thus Walter J. LaBuy, who became the first Polish American federal judge, had planned for a legal career since high school. After completion of law school, he served an apprenticeship as assistant city attorney in Carter Harrison's last administration. He then

---

[5]*Dziennik Zjednoczenia,* February 12, 1929, translated as part of the Federal Writers Project in the Works Progress Administration and available on microfilm at the Chicago Public Library under the title *Chicago Foreign Language Press Survey* (CFLPS), Polish section, II-B-3. Also, *Chicago Daily News,* November 1, 1930, p. 7; personal interviews with Charles Rozmarek, former Polish National Alliance president; Stanley Piotrowicz, realtor; Congressman Daniel Rostenkowski; Peter Figel, precinct captain; Walter Nega, personal secretary to Congressman Rostenkowski.

practiced law privately for fifteen years, served two terms as a Cook County commissioner at the beginning of the Depression, and finally in 1933 was elected a judge of the circuit court. Ten years later, the Roosevelt administration, on the advice of Mayor Kelly, raised LaBuy to the federal bench. When Thaddeus Adesko, a younger lawyer than LaBuy, had his heart set on a judgeship in the 1940's, his ward boss (an Irishman) arranged the terms with Mayor Kelly—first, two terms for Adesko in the state senate, then a judgeship. Both Adesko and Kelly kept their side of the bargain, and Judge Adesko steadily rose in the ranks of the judiciary.[6]

Judge Edmund K. Jarecki was the most noteworthy member of the respectable camp in the twenties and thirties, and he was occasionally trumpeted by Polonia as a potential mayoral candidate. Particularly after his successful defiance of the Kelly-Nash machine in 1938, many thought he should have struck for wider power in the following year's mayoral race. But such suggestions fundamentally misread both Jarecki and the political situation.

Jarecki's experience had been legal and judicial, not political. He was not a power-seeker, he had no desire to run for mayor, and he might not have been an altogether credible candidate if he had. He had thoroughly alienated the ward bosses of Chicago and would not easily have united the bosses' muscle with his own respectability. Besides, the Kelly-Nash machine, though it had made two blunders, was not about to crumble at the attack of respectables alone. Democratic Governor Henry Horner in 1936 and Jarecki in 1938 had been able to hold their offices because they were well-known, respected incumbents dumped gratuitously by an arrogant Cook County Democratic machine. If Jarecki had challenged Mayor Kelly in 1939, however, the situation would have been reversed. He would have been trying to eliminate a popular and successful incumbent and would have been open to charges of personal arrogance, opportunism, and vindictiveness. Thomas Courtney's crushing primary defeat by Mayor Kelly in 1939 indicates what Jarecki's fate would have been had he made the attempt himself.

Judge Jarecki and the other Polish respectables knew enough about politics to cooperate with the machine and attain the capstone of a legal career, a seat on the bench. They were respected in both Polish American and wider circles as honest, worthy, professional men; but they were not power-seekers. Edmund

---

[6]"Report to the Chicago Bar Association," May 15, 1939, and assorted newspaper clippings, in Walter J. LaBuy papers, University of Illinois at Chicago Circle; personal interview, Judge Thaddeus Adesko.

Jarecki spoke for all of them in summing up his own career:

"It has been my contention that the duties and responsibilities of the county judgeship are primarily judicial—not political—though they involve control and supervision of what commonly has been called the 'election machinery'. . .

"I have never kept silent on the subject of election frauds even when it would have been 'good politics' to keep quiet. However, everyone knows by common report that 'Jarecki is a bad politician but a lucky fellow.' " Such lucky fellows could have prestigious careers, but they could not and did not fight for the mayoralty.[7]

The second generation in Polonia's capital did produce two men, Matt Szymczak and Benjamin Adamowski, who seemed to have the proper combination of political ability and respectable appeal to reach for the mayoral chair; but both, for very different reasons, disqualified themselves along the way.

Matt Szymczak (1894-1978) was clearly the leading Polish American in Chicago politics in the early thirties. He held one of the top positions in Mayor Cermak's inner circle; had Cermak lived to complete one or more successful terms, Szymczak might well have been the heir-apparent. But even after the Czech mayor's death, Szymczak's position remained strong. City controller, ward committeeman on the North West side, and managing director of Chicago's Polish American Democratic Organization (PADO), founded in 1932, he was the leading voice of the organized Polish Americans in city politics. Not yet forty years old in 1933, he had time to wait out Mayor Kelly's long tenure in office. As a banker, professor, and businessman, he had the administrative skill and businesslike reputation needed to win the respectable vote. With the actual strength of a ward base and the potential ethnic strength of PADO, he had political muscle as well. As an old precinct captain has phrased it, "Szymczak knew how to speak to bankers in their language and how to speak to the people in the language of the streets."

But his 1933 appointment to the Federal Reserve Board effectively removed him from the political scene. Many in Polonia later viewed this appointment as a shrewd move by the Irish leadership to kick Szymczak upstairs and thus eliminate a serious rival. That this was the actual intention is doubtful. The Irish bosses did not initiate negotiations for this appointment; President-elect Roosevelt himself first made the offer of a position to Szymczak while Mayor Cermak was still alive. Szymczak welcomed the

[7]*Chicago Daily News*, October 20, 1936, p. 4.

appointment for both personal and professional reasons, happy to remove his family from the burdensome milieu of ward politics and eager to exercise his financial skill at the highest levels. Nevertheless, Szymczak's acceptance removed him from politics as effectively as a kick upstairs. Though possessing far more political potential than John Smulski had, Szymczak, like Smulski, ultimately chose to abandon active politics for more prestigious, respectable activities; and Polonia's capital thus lost an important political opportunity.[8]

Benjamin Adamowski did not abandon politics for a nonpolitical post, but rather left the security of the regular party ranks for a career as a political maverick. Considered a "boy wonder" in his early years, Adamowski was admitted to the Illinois bar at the age of twenty-one. With the help of Clayton F. Smith, his ward leader and a second father to him after the death of his own father, alderman Max Adamowski, young Ben went to the state legislature in 1930, still only twenty-three years old. Loyal at first to the Cermak and then the Kelly-Nash leadership, he became majority leader of the legislature in 1935.

Though temperamentally combative and something of a maverick even during these early years in the legislature, he did not oppose the Chicago machine leadership on any issue of importance until 1938, when Judge Jarecki was abandoned by the machine and by the Polish American Democratic Organization. In that year Adamowski made his first break with the machine. He was one of the few important Polish Democrats to stand by the judge.

At a contentious PADO meeting early in 1938, Adamowski challenged the submissiveness of the organization to machine dictates, bitterly asking, "If the Polish organization refused to give its support to a judge like Jarecki, how can it maintain that it exists only for the good of the Polish people?" Adamowski was later expelled from PADO along with Jarecki; he then began a long career of independence, alternately opposing and making his peace with the Democratic machine, then finally breaking with it altogether and switching parties.

Adamowski retained his seat in the legislature until 1941 on the basis of his own strength in his heavily Polish district; and for a little

[8]Personal interviews, Aloysius Mazewski, PNA president; Charles Piatkiewicz, former editor of *Dziennik Związkowy;* Frank Bobrytzke, former PADO president; Peter Figel, precinct captain; Walter Nega, secretary to Congressman Rostenkowski; Matthew Bieszczat, county commissioner and former PADO president. All of these individuals stressed that Szymczak was the man most likely to be Chicago's first Polish mayor; many of them blamed the Irish for "kicking him upstairs." In a personal interview, M. S. Szymczak denied that he was kicked upstairs, and the sequence of events supports this.

over a year after 1938, he also served as attorney for the Board of Election Commissioners, a reward from the grateful Judge Jarecki. He unsuccessfully challenged the machine candidate for US Senator in the 1940 Democratic primary, then ran two years later, equally unsuccessfully, for Illinois congressman-at-large with machine backing. After several periods of private law practice and a three-year stint as city corporation counsel under Mayor Martin Kennelly in the late forties, he resumed his maverick role in 1955, futilely challenging Richard J. Daley for the mayoral nomination to succeed Kennelly. Thereafter, he switched parties; as a Republican, he was elected Cook County state's attorney in 1956, using his full talents as a controversial battler in this crime-fighting office. In 1963, as the Republican candidate for mayor, he held Richard Daley to his smallest margin of victory. As recently as November of 1970, he was still battling the Daley machine, unsuccessfully running on the Republican ticket for county assessor.[9]

From the standpoint of political power in Chicago, Benjamin Adamowski's career was another lost opportunity for Polonia's capital. Even younger than Szymczak, he too had time to wait and work his way up in the organization. He also had political connections—his early rise to house leadership at the age of twenty-eight attests to that—and a reputation as an honest, aggressive lawyer which might have jelled into the proper political combination for a successful mayoral bid. But his frequent bouts of "irregularity" made him anathema to party leaders, killing any chance of a regular party nomination for mayor; and the great strength of the Democratic machine in Chicago since the thirties similarly doomed his independent and Republican bids for the mayoralty.

Democrats in Polonia's capital feel that Adamowski could have been mayor had he not been "impatient." Adamowski's tilting at machine windmills came from both a sensitive conscience and a stubborn personality. He fought the machine both out of principle and because he seems to have enjoyed fighting almost for its own sake. An early experience in the state legislature may have determined much of his later conduct. When he first arrived in Springfield in 1931, Michael Igoe, the Democratic floor leader, told him he was starting off with two strikes against him because his Polish predecessors in the legislature had made a bad record. Adamowski asserts that, then and there, he vowed to prove that a

---

[9]PADO minutes, February 5, 1938; biography of Adamowski, *Chicago Daily News*, February 7, 1955, in PADO papers; Mike Royko, *Boss: Richard J. Daley of Chicago* (New York: E. P. Dutton and Co., 1971), pp. 85, 98, 119.

Pole could be honest, capable, and intelligent in public office. This incident seems to have left a permanent chip on his shoulder. He himself has few regrets and has summed up his career thus: "Swimming downstream is easy and pleasant, but it doesn't compare with the exhilaration of swimming upstream and fighting the currents and rapids." Nevertheless, his "impatience" did destroy his early promise as a political "comer"; for Polonia, it meant another lost opportunity.[10]

Such opportunities for Polonia were few. From the second generation, only Szymczak and Adamowski seemed to have the potential for leadership in the city's politics; and the occasions on which they might have made a mayoral bid occurred infrequently. The Irish came to dominate Chicago politics at a rather late date, compared to other Democratic cities; but when they finally solidified their dominance in the early thirties, it remained paramount at a time when Irish leaders of other cities saw power slipping away.

Only two occasions have presented themselves between 1933 and 1976 when a non-Irish leader might have made a bid for City Hall: in 1947 when Ed Kelly finally retired amid charges of bossism and rumors of corruption, and in 1955 when the honest successor to Kelly, Martin Kennelly, was eased out of office as a political weakling. At either of these junctures, Szymczak or Adamowski might well have become mayor had they retained an active, regular party presence in Chicago. But since then no opportunities have arisen, for Richard Daley and his machine have proven politically invincible. Why was Polonia's capital so unsuccessful at producing a leader in the Cermak mold, who could seize political power in the city and give decisive proof that his ethnic group had arrived?

It may have been simply long odds and bad luck. The obstacles against a new immigrant politician rising to power in a large, heterogeneous city should not be down-played. Only the highly unusual situation of Big Bill Thompson's utter degradation allowed Cermak to win in Chicago in 1931. In New York City in 1933, Fiorello LaGuardia achieved a victory similar to Cermak's, using his skills as a broker, his ambition for power, and his passion for reform to become the first Italian American mayor of that city. But again, only a major scandal and an internal crumbling of the Tammany machine allowed him to win a fusion victory. Victories like LaGuardia's and Cermak's have been rare for new immigrant

[10]Personal interviews, Thaddeus Adesko, Matthew Bieszczat, Daniel Rostenkowski, Benjamin Adamowski.

groups, and the elements of sheer luck and unique personalities cannot be discounted.[11]

Yet there may be deeper reasons for Polonia's failure to elect a mayor than mere chance. Polish Americans themselves have suggested a number of reasons. Those of a Polish National Alliance persuasion have often berated Polonia for its bloc Democratic voting. The Alliance papers repeatedly implored Chicago's Poles to break their one party allegiance, so that both parties would take them seriously, and to adopt a "swing vote" or "balance of power" strategy, voting for the man or the party which does the most for the group. Such a strategy might have gained Polonia more attention and a bit more patronage, as both parties found they could not take the Polish vote for granted; but it is unlikely that it would have led to more political power or to a Polish mayor. In the 1920's and 30's, when Polonia was first striking for wider recognition, the Republican party in Chicago was a dying institution; and it has been all but dead since then. Neither a total defection of all Polish voters nor an occasional defection of half the Polish voters to the Republicans would have revived their fortunes. And dividing the Polish vote in this way would have lessened the chances of capturing the Democratic party. Furthermore, if Cermak and LaGuardia are taken as models of successful ethnic politics, it appears that bloc voting is no disadvantage. LaGuardia used his life-long Republicanism and Cermak the bloc Democratic vote of the Czechs as one element in the climb to power. Not a bloc vote, but the failure to move out from this base seems more pertinent to Polonia's failure.

Polish Americans, also, have privately blamed their own tendency towards factionalism for their lack of political success. This trait is supposedly imbedded deep in the national character and calls up ghosts of the *liberum veto* in the Polish Diet and the anarchic individualism of Poland's *szlachta*. Factionalism has certainly been a hindrance in particular local contests, most notably in the drive to elect Polonia's first congressman. Anarchic individualism and inability to work in harness, another side of the legendary Polish factionalism, also describes Ben Adamowski's maverick career quite well. Perhaps this trait in Polish and Polish American culture, which militates against patient, disciplined, broker politics, has been a factor in limiting Polish American political success.

[11]See Arthur Mann, *LaGuardia Comes to Power* (Philadelphia: J. B. Lippincott Co., 1965), for the story of LaGuardia's election in 1933.

But a more fundamental factor, I believe, prevented the recognition drive from reaching completion in a Polish American mayor. The whole thrust of ethnic politics as pursued by the Polish Americans during the recognition drive and as practiced by other ethnic and racial groups in American politics was probably misguided. Ethnic politics, when it means closing ranks in group solidarity and seeking power as a distinct, separate group, has severe limitations. It only succeeds when the group forms a majority of the voters in a political division. Even then, success is not often taken seriously by others; for the group's leaders are then thought of as "big fish in a small pond." Success in larger, more pluralist, sectors of American politics must be coalition, broker politics.

Polonia's capital suffered from the ironic disadvantage of being the largest new immigrant group in Chicago yet falling well short of a numerical majority in the city. Their relatively large numbers were a disadvantage in two ways: they nurtured the illusion that if Polish voters would only stick together they could gain power and importance in politics by sheer weight of numbers; second, they made other new groups consider the Polish community a threat. Had they been more numerous or the city smaller, Polish Americans could have eventually dominated politics in Chicago as they did in the small city of Hamtramck, Michigan.[12] Were they less numerous, they might have recognized their marginality and played a broker's role as Cermak's Czechs did. But, as it was, they were a prey to their own illusions and a target of other groups' jealousies.

A major Polish language daily, *Dziennik Chicagoski,* at the time of Mayor Cermak's death, warned against the illusions inherent in Polonia's large numbers:

A Pole will be mayor of Chicago, only if we continue the politics of the dead Mayor Cermak, i.e., if we make alliances with other groups . . . Unfortunately, the majority among us is now playing at Pan-Slavism and forgetting that Mayor Cermak practiced a different kind of politics. In his organization were found next to the Czechs, Jews; next to the Poles, Irish; next to the Germans, Swedes.[13]

However, neither the *Chicagoski* nor the other Polish leaders seem to have taken this advice to heart. Led by PADO, Polish politicans continued to act as if political power would fall to Polonia like a ripe fruit, if only it could perfect its own unity and solidarity.

The political experience of New York's ethnic groups confirms the disadvantage inherent in large numbers which fall short of a

---

[12]Arthur Evans Wood, *Hamtramck* (New Haven, Conn.: College and University Press, 1955), pp. 46-114, discusses the factionalism of Polish American politics in Hamtramck and the city's low reputation in the greater Detroit area.
[13]*Dziennik Chicagoski,* March 14, 1933, p. 4.

majority. Just as Chicago's Poles form the city's largest ethnic group in the twentieth century, yet have never elected a mayor, so too New York's Jews are clearly that city's largest community, but the first Jewish mayor of New York was elected only recently, in 1973. Not a Jew, but LaGuardia, representing the smaller Italian community of New York, was the first to crack the WASP and Irish monopoly in city politics.

For newly emergent groups, solidarity politics is probably a necessary first step; but it reaches a point of diminishing returns. Only through coalition politics, broker politics, the politics of painful compromise and careful bridge-building can a new group be succesful at the highest levels in pluralist, polyglot America. Polish American politicians were dedicated to the Polonia ideal of strength in unity. But in a pluralist society, politics must go beyond the internal unity of one group. The role of politics is to unify all groups in a society, to manage conflicts between groups.

The successful ethnic leader is the one who builds bridges across the hyphen—not a *Polish*—American but a Polish American.[14] Matt Szymczak probably realized this, and his long service on the Federal Reserve Board, though it removed him from political contention in Chicago, cannot be called a failure. He served his country and his ancestral community well. Had there been more Szymczaks, some would have won prominence in Chicago and others would have gone on to other areas as he did. But too many of his compatriots tried to use the hyphen as a bludgeon rather than a bridge. Polonia's capital remained in the stage of hyphenated politics too long. Why this was so cannot be explained completely without going further into the murky depths of national character. But certainly Polonia's difficult numerical position in Chicago, neither a small, hungry minority nor a clear, dominant majority, has had much to do with its failure to elect a Chicago mayor.

Polonia's capital may not get another opportunity. Among the third generation of Polish American politicians (men who entered politics after World War II and are active today), only one seems to have the potential combination needed for a mayoral bid in the post-Daley era—Congressman Daniel Rostenkowski. Son of the old ward boss Joe Rosty, Daniel Rostenkowski succeeded his father as thirty-second ward committeeman, is widely recognized as the Chicago machine's legislative representative in the US Congress,

---

[14] I am greatly indebted, in my discussion of hyphenization and broker politics, to Arthur Mann's analysis of LaGuardia as a "marginal man", a political hybrid, and a "balanced ticket all by himself" in *LaGuardia Comes to Power*, pp. 24-27.

and is sometimes mentioned as a possible Daley successor. He has both machine connections and a "bright young man" image which could conceivably make him a strong contender for the mayoralty. Yet he has been building up seniority in Congress from a safe seat (a "civil service congressman," as one politician called him); and there is, at present, no certainty he would be willing to risk this position in a struggle for city power with Daley's other heirs.[15]

Ethnic groups move into and out of power in American cities in a fairly regular succession. Old-stock Americans gave way to the Irish, who, in turn, have been challenged by the newer immigrant groups when they became numerous. But as Congressman Rostenkowski himself has said, Poles had better move fast if they wish to take their turn at the helm in Chicago's City Hall; for the "next group up," the blacks, are growing ever more numerous in the city and have begun to elect mayors in other northern cities. It may well be that, because of the lack of a suitable leader in the second generation, when they were the next group up, Chicago's Polish Americans never will elect one of their own as mayor.[16]

[15]Editor's note: Rostenkowski did not seek the Democratic party's mayoral nomination in the special primary election held on April 19, 1977 to fill the post left vacant with Richard J. Daley's death on December 28, 1976. Instead, he together with most of the Polish Americans in the Cook County party organization backed the winning candidacy of Acting Mayor Michael Bilandic, a long-time Daley favorite, a Croation American, and previously the alderman representing the city ward district where Daley had resided. Bilandic received 342,000 votes and a plurality in 39 of the city's 50 wards, later easily defeating a weak Republican challenge in the general election.

A Polish American, alderman Roman Pucinski, for many years a party organization loyalist and a one-time US Congressman, did challenge the party and captured 218,000 votes, finishing a distant second to Bilandic in a field of six candidates. Significantly, Pucinski won in only seven of Chicago's Polish wards and all these were located on the North and Northwest sections of the city, the areas earlier represented by Pucinski in Congress. He failed to win in any other part of the city where large numbers of Polish Americans were concentrated. For information on the election see the *Chicago Tribune*, April 21, 1977, p. 6; and the map in the appendix to this work.

Daley's power base had been the two offices he had held since the early 1950's, one the mayorship, the other the chairmanship of the Cook County Democratic party. After his death Bilandic was elected mayor, but the post of party chairman went to an Irish American, George Dunne. Polish American party loyalists had to be satisfied with the selection of alderman Casimir Laskowski to a newly-created ceremonial office of vice mayor.

[16]See Robert A. Dahl, *Who Governs?* (New Haven, Conn.: Yale University Press, 1961), and Donald S. Bradley and Mayer N. Zald, "From Commercial Elite to Political Administrator," *American Journal of Sociology*, 70 (September 1965), 153-67, for typologies of the succession of various kinds of mayors. Bradley and Zald, dealing specifically with Chicago, divided the mayors into the following chronological and typological categories: commercial elite (1837-68); transition mayors (1868-75); personalized politics vs. party machine (1876-1930); political administrators (1931-   ). Though the authors do not emphasize the ethnic origins of the mayors, it is clear that both the commercial elite and the transition mayors were WASPs; the battle between personalized politics and party machine was a battle between individual WASPs (the two Harrisons and Thompson) and an Irish clique; and the political administrators, with the exception of the first, Cermak, were all Irish. It is during this last period that the new immigrants were the next group up. To succeed in this type of politics, a mayor would have to practice broker politics among many differing groups.

Name Index

Adamkiewicz, Stanley 95
Adamowski, Benjamin 11, 98-102
Adamowski, Max 99
Adesko, Thaddeus 97, 101n
Atkielski, Bishop Roman 72
Austin, Richard 59
Bahorski, Jozef 51
Banfield, Edward 30
Berger, Victor 85
Bielewski, Albert 51
Bieszczat, Matthew 99n, 101n
Bilandic, Michael 11, 105
Blenski, Michael 68, 83n
Bobrowicz, Edmund 76-7
Bobrytzke, Frank 99n
Borchardt, Francis 79
Bradley, Donald 105n
Brennan, George 93
Brophy, John 77
Bryan, William Jennings 42
Budny, Stanley 66n
Bunge, William 63n
Carter, James E. 53
Carter, Lawrence 61n
Catlin, George 63
Celichowski, Stanley 89n
Cermak, Anton 92-4, 96, 98,
                          101-3, 105n
Choinski, Edmund 66n
Clancy, Robert 51-2
Coolidge, Calvin 20
Courtney, Thomas 97
Couzens, James 47n
Crangle, Joseph 27, 34
Crotty, Peter 25-27
Cybulski, Stanley, ... 90n
Cyrowski, August 44, 45n, 47
Czerwinski, Joseph 83n
Czerwinski, Roman 81
Dahl, Robert 30, 84
Daley, Richard 11, 100-1, 104-5
Davis, Glenn 83
Debs, Eugene 71
Deptula, Szymon 66n
Diggs, Charles 60
Dingell, John 53
Dingell, John, Jr. 53, 59n
Dunn, George 105n
Drzewieniecki, Walter 38n

Dziengelewski, Jozef 51
Eisenhower, Dwight 71
Epstein, Leon 90
Eve, Arthur 22
Farrell, Thomas 44
Figel, Peter 96n, 99n
Fitzgerald, Governor 59n
Foley, Bishop 63n
Ford, Gerald 73
Ford, Henry 47n, 48, 55, 56, 61
Foreman, Harry 28
Friedlander, Peter 56n, 57n
Gawin, August 81
Gebert, Boleslaw 55n
Glazer, Nathan 31n, 38
Goral, Rev. Boleslaus 72
Gorecki, Martin 70
Gordon, Thomas 96
Gottfried, Alex 93n
Greeley, Andrew 7n, 13n, 78n
Greene, Victor 43n, 76n
Greenstone, J.D. 65n
Gregorski, Francis 83n
Gribbs, Roman 59, 60, 64, 65
Griffin, James 22
Gulski, Rev. Hyacinth 72
Harrison, Carter 92, 96, 105n
Hauser, Philip 13
Hawkins, Brett 16n
Hecock, Donald 52n
Hicks, Louise 29
Hillary, John 22, 25
Hoan, Daniel 81n, 85, 88
Hoover, Herbert 51
Horner, Henry 97
Horski, Francis 19
Hudson, J.L. 47n
Humphrey, Hubert 23, 53
Igoe, Michael 100
Jankowski, Cass 51
Jankowski, Harold 66n
Janiszewski family 70
Jarecki, Edmund 97-9
Jasnowski, Adolph 42n
Jezewski, Peter 49
Johnson (Jasiek), Jacob 19
Johnson, Lyndon 53
Kalupa, John 66n, 81, 86n
Kaszubowski, Joseph 24

Katzban, Michael 70
Kelly, Edward 95-8, 101
Kelly, K.T. 56
Kendziorski, Casimir 88
Kennedy, John 53
Kennelly, Martin 11, 100-1
Kleczka, Gerald 88
Kleczka, John 52, 80, 81, 83n, 86
Knowles, Warren 83
Kohler, William 83
Kolowich, George 51
Koltunski, Casimir 89n
Konkel, X. 44n, 45n
Konkowski, Frank 95
Kopernik (Copernicus) 77-8
Kosciuszko, Thaddeus 75
Kotecki, Louis 81
Kowal, Chester 23, 25, 26
Kozlowski, Bishop Edward 72, 76
Krawczyk, Edmund 89n
Kristalski, George 58
Kronk, Adam 54n
Kronk, John 50, 59
Kruszka, Michael 9, 67, 70, 72-3, 76, 79, 80, 86
Kruszka, Rev. Wenceslaus 9, 67, 72, 78, 79
Krzycki, Leo 68, 71, 76, 77n, 86
Kunz, Stanley 52, 94, 95
LaBuy, Walter 96-7
La Follette, Philip 86
La Follette, Robert M. 71, 82, 86
LaGuardia, Fiorello 101-2, 104
Lane, Robert 7, 30
Laskowski, Casimir 105n
Lemke, Felix 42n
Lesinski, John 53
Lesinski, John, Jr. 53n, 59n
Lesinski, T. John 59n
Lewandowski, Mieczyslaw 64
Lodge, John 47n
Lopata, Helena 84
Lorinskas, Robert 16n, 19n
Lubell, Samuel 20
Lux, Elmer 25
Machrowicz, Thaddeus 45
Madaj. Rev. M.J. 15
Maier, Henry 83n
Mann, Arthur 102n, 104n
Manz, Victor 25-6
Makowski, Stanley 22, 23, 27n

Mazewski, Aloysius 99n
McCarthy, Joseph 82
McGovern, George 53, 59n
Michalski, Clemens 66n, 82, 90n
Michalski, Edward 82
Michalski, Joseph 82
Miech, Robert 83
Moynihan, Daniel 31n, 38
Mruk, Joseph 22, 23, 25, 28
Muskie, Edmund 21
Nedzi, Lucien 53n
Nega, Walter 96n, 99n
Nichols, Charles 44
Nixon, Richard 71
Nowak, Stanley 55n, 58, 61n
Nowakowski, Richard B. 82, 89n
Nowakowski, Richard C. 82
Nowicki, Leo 59, 65
O'Konski, Alvin 82-3
Ostrowski, M. 44n
Pankow, Steve 22, 25
Parenti, Michael 19n
Pawinski, Peter 81
Peck, George 81
Piatkiewicz, Charles 99n
Pingree, Hazen 42-3
Piotrowicz, Stanley 96n
Piotrowski, N.L. 96
Pitass, Rev. John 18
Plewa, John 66n
Polakowski, John 66n
Polakowski, Walter 68, 71, 86
Proxmire, William 83
Pruss, Thaddeus 66n, 83n
Przybylo, Joseph 95
Pucinski, Roman 11, 105
Pulaski, Casimir, ... 75
Remigia (Napolska), S.M. 41, 42n
Renkiewicz, Frank 15
Reuss, Henry 83n
Rhode, Bishop Paul 45
Robinson, Edgar 52n
Roosevelt, Franklin 20, 24, 52, 86
Rose, David 88
Rostenkowski, Daniel 11, 96n, 99n, 101n, 104, 105
Rostenkowski, Joseph 95-9, 104
Rozan, Jacob 19
Rozmarek, Charles 96n
Rudzinski, August 79
Rudzinski, Theodore 79

Sadowski, George 53
Schmandt, Henry 79
Sedita, Frank 23, 25, 26, 27, 29n
Seidel, Emil 85, 88
Skrzycki, S. 44n
Skwierawski, Michael 83
Slominski, Alfreda 23, 29, 30
Smietanka, Julius 96
Smith, Al 20, 51, 52, 71
Smith, Clayton 99
Smulski, John 94, 96
Sosnowski, John 51-2
Stanislawski, Emil 89n
Stevenson, Adlai 53
Still, Bayrd 79n
Swietlik, Francis X. 66n, 68, 83n
Szymczak, Anthony 66n
Szymczak, Matt 98-9, 100, 101, 104
Temple, Donald 15
Tenerowicz, Rudolph 53n
Thompson, William ... 92, 94, 101, 105n
Tillman, Henry 41
Tobiasz, Raymond 88
Tomasik, Edward 66n
Trojanowski, Mrs. 56

Truman, Harry 24n, 53
Tuczynski, Philip 66n
Ulinski, John 24, 25
Van Wagoner, Governor 59n
Wabiszewski family 70
Wallace, George 21
Waner, John 11
Wasielewski, Thaddeus 76, 77, 81, 83n, 88
White, Fred 56
White, Theodore 25
Wierzbicki, Anthony 59
Wilson, James Q. 30
Wilson, Woodrow 77
Wolfinger, Raymond 30, 31n
Wood, Arthur 41n, 103n
York, Joe (Jurkiewicz) 57
Young, Coleman 60
Zablocki, Clement 65, 77, 81-3, 88
Zablocki, Thomas 83n
Zaborski, Richard 83
Zald, Mayer 105n
Zeidler, Frank 66n, 82, 83n
Zintak, Frank 96
Zuk, Mary 57-8

APPENDICES

APPENDIX 1a

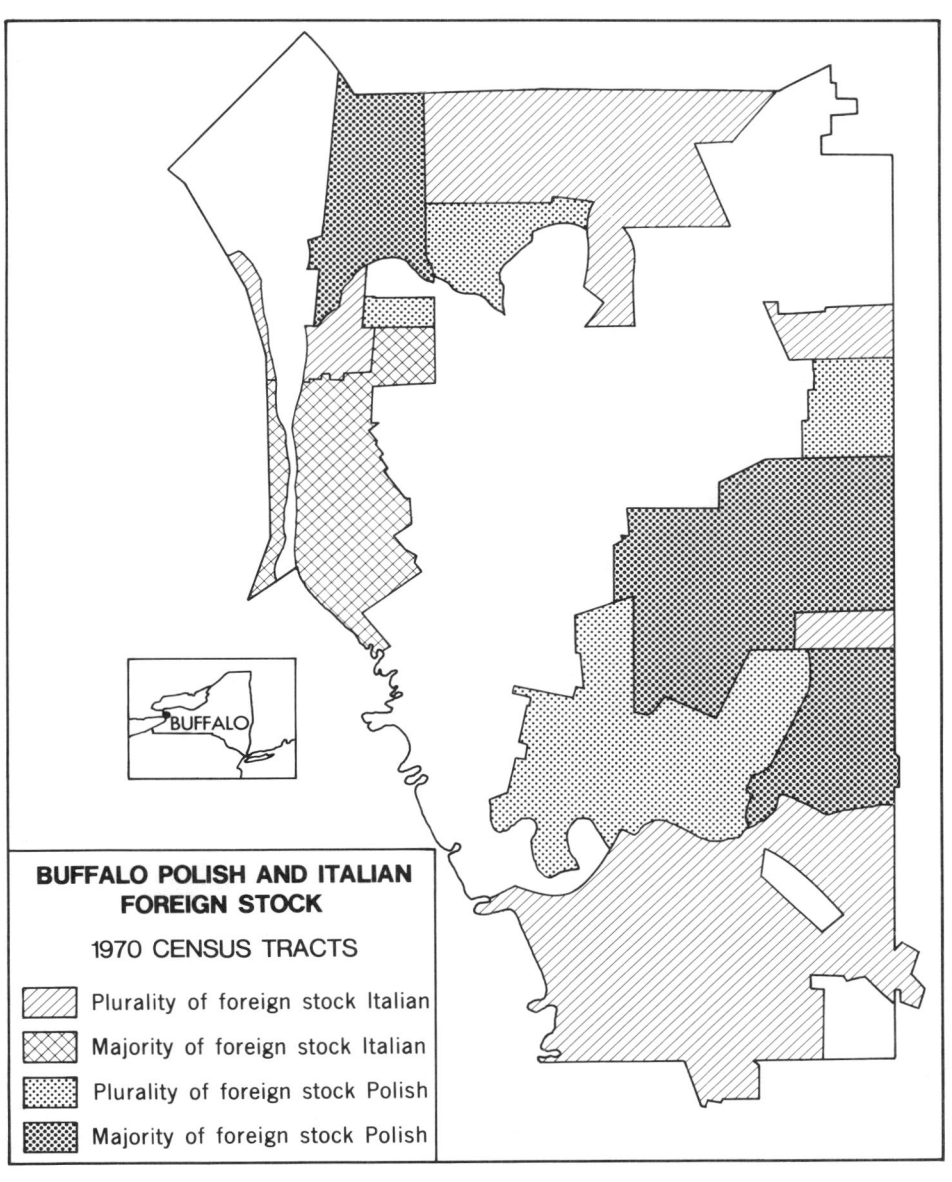

APPENDIX 1b

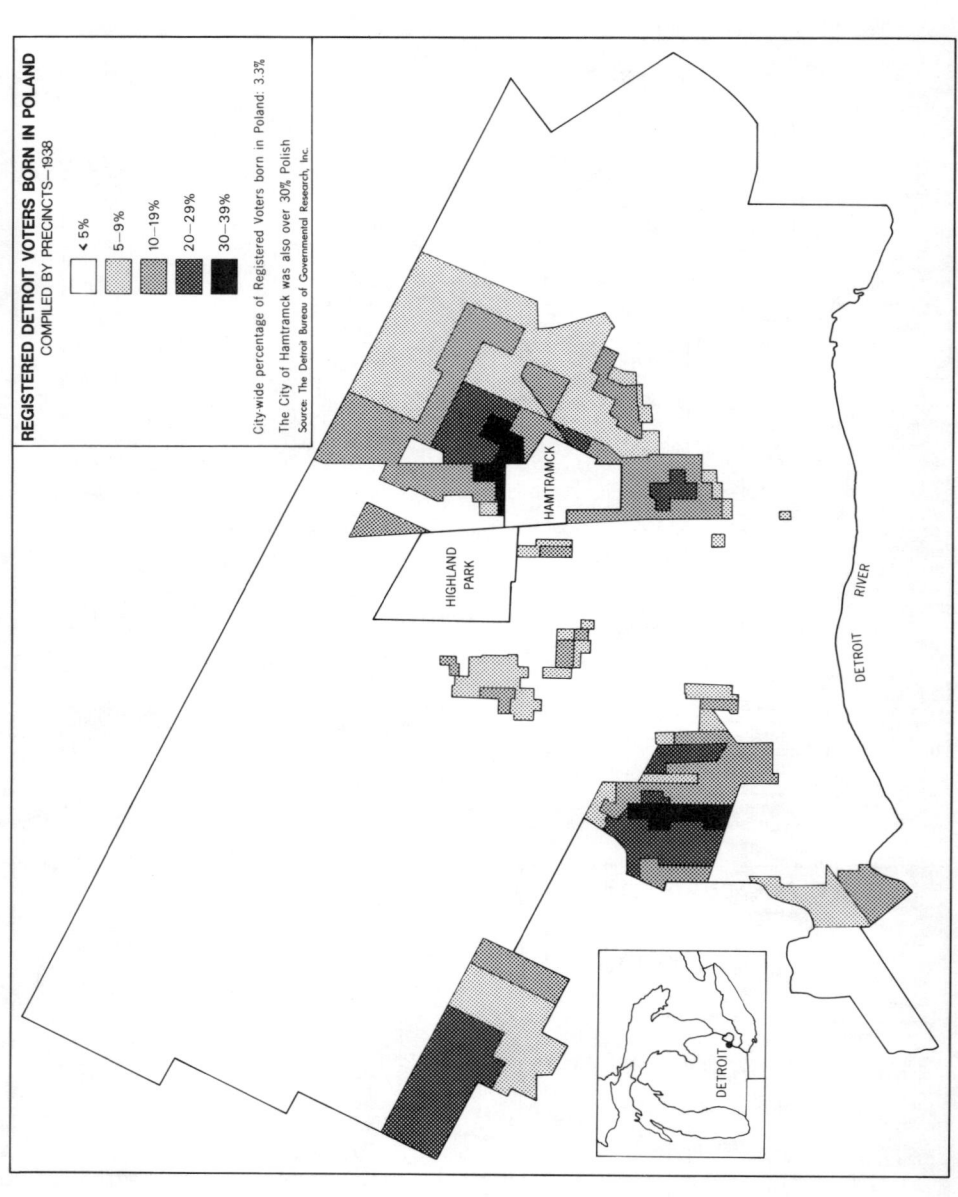

APPENDIX 1c

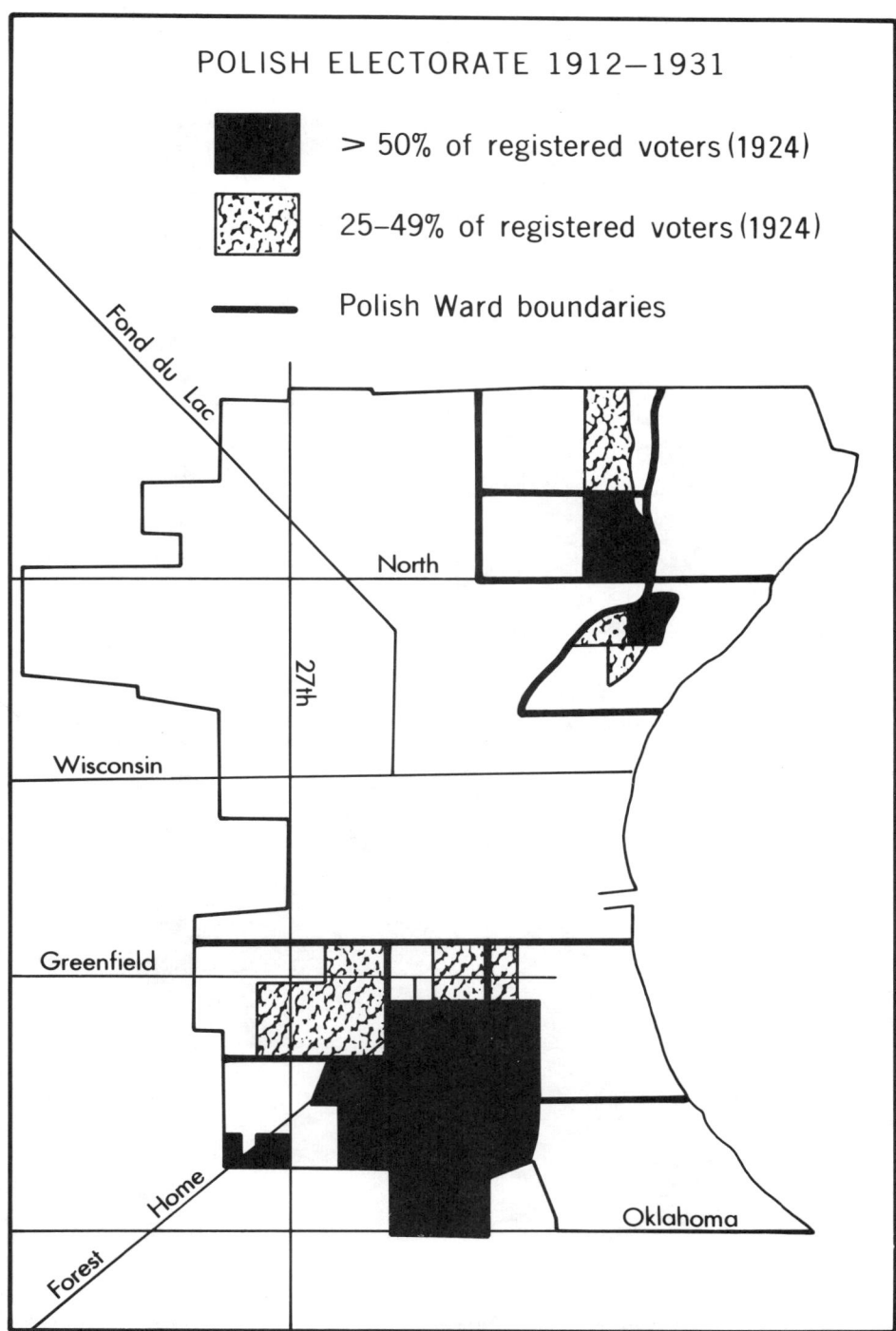

APPENDIX 1d

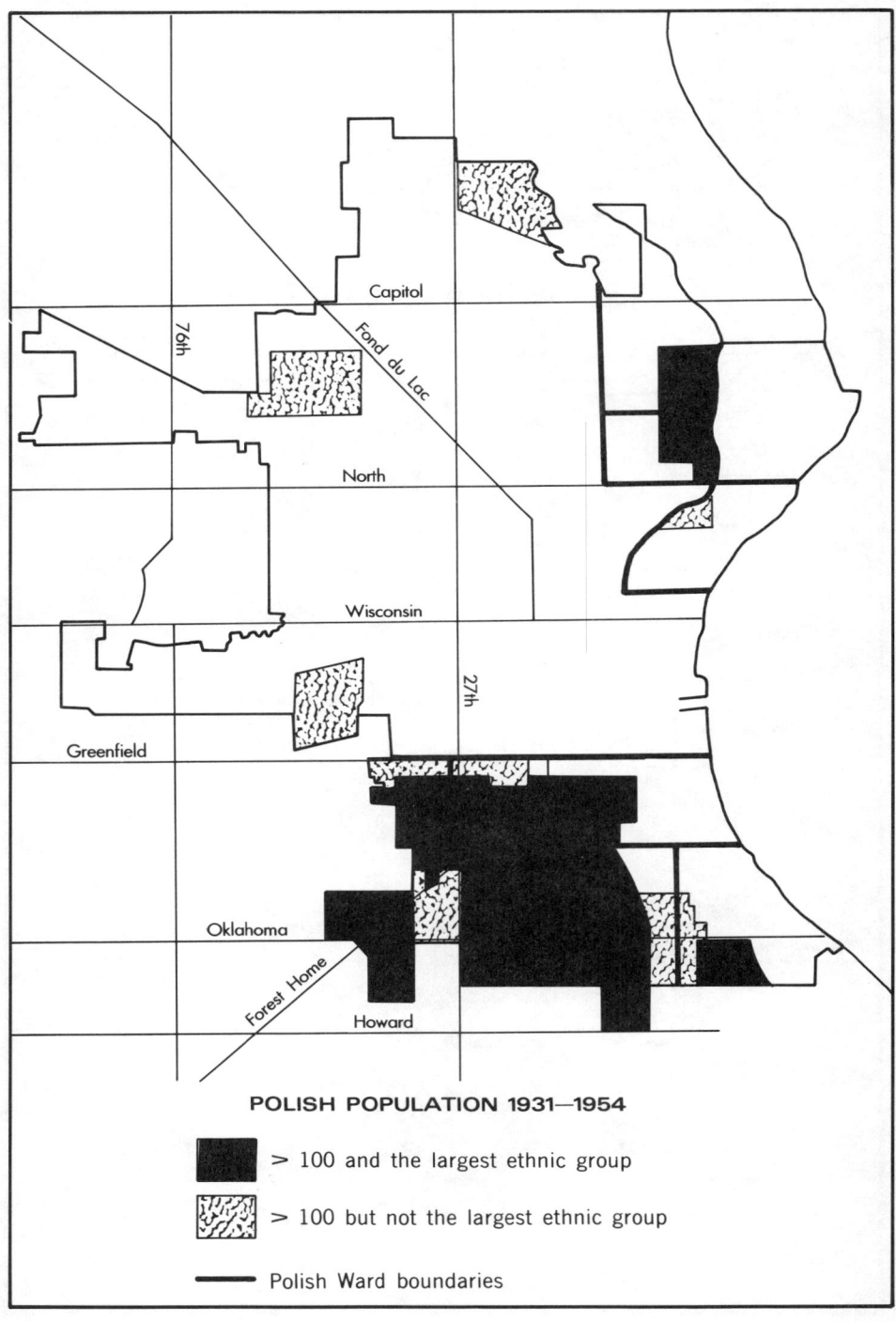

APPENDIX 1e

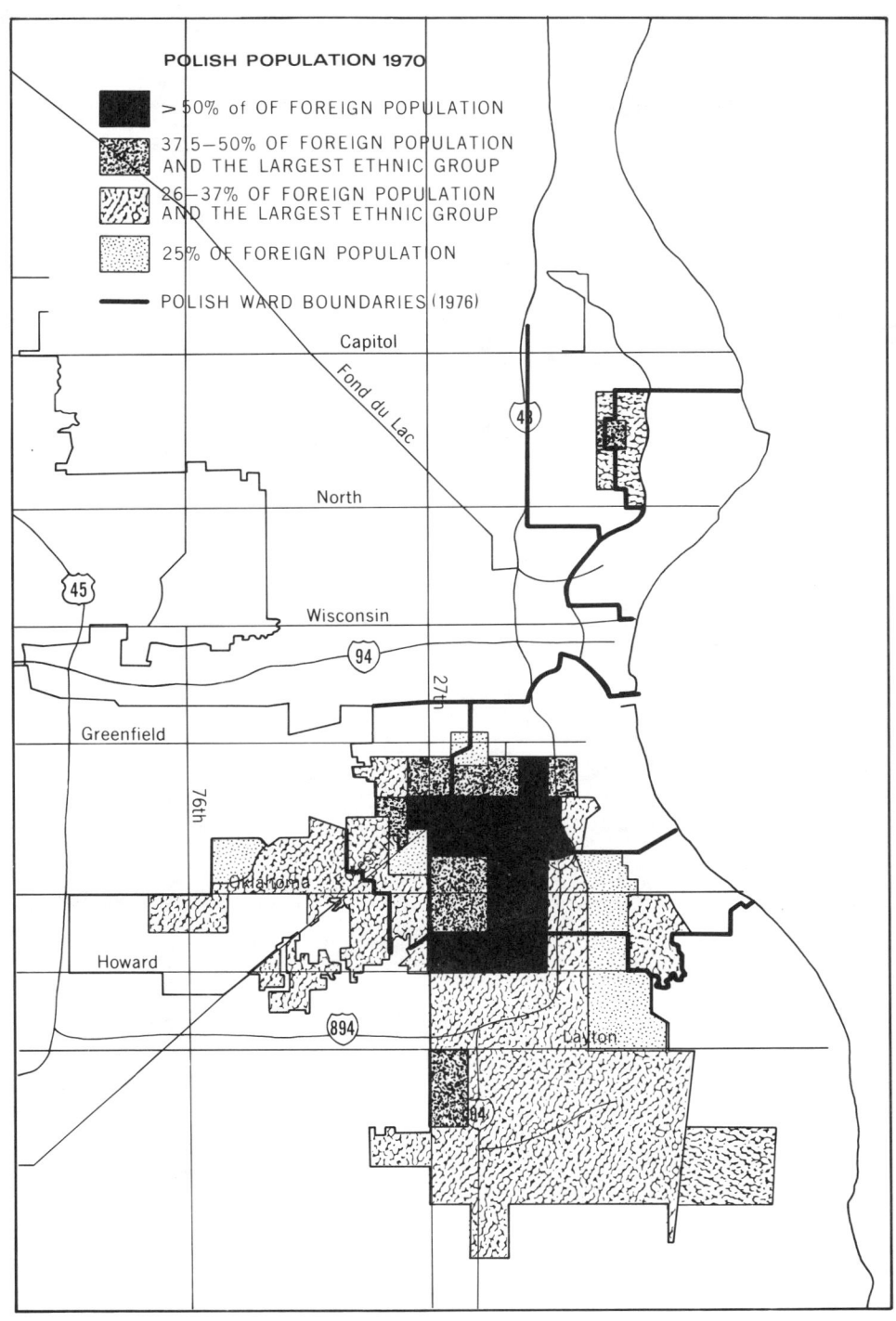

APPENDIX 1f

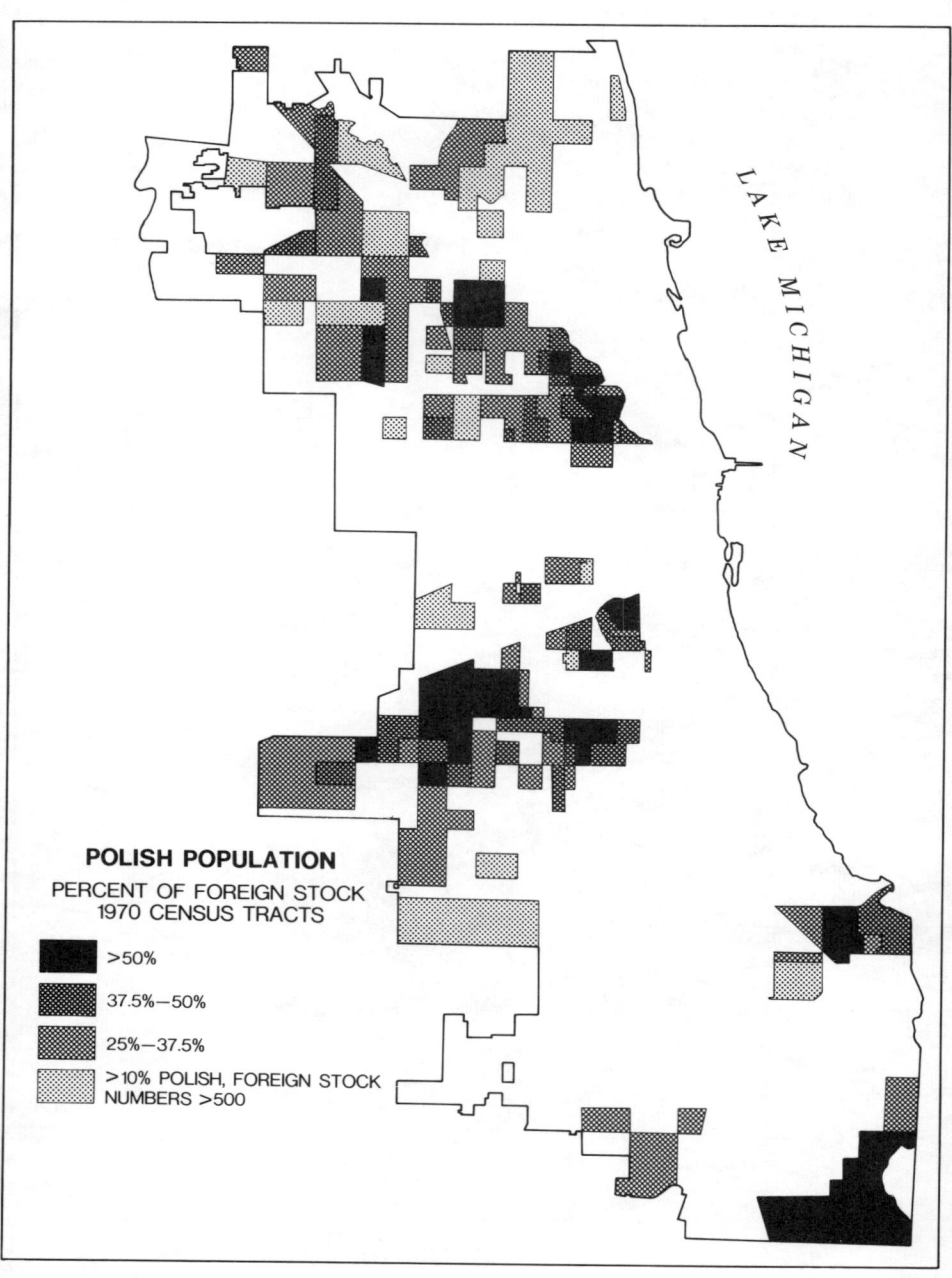

APPENDIX 1g

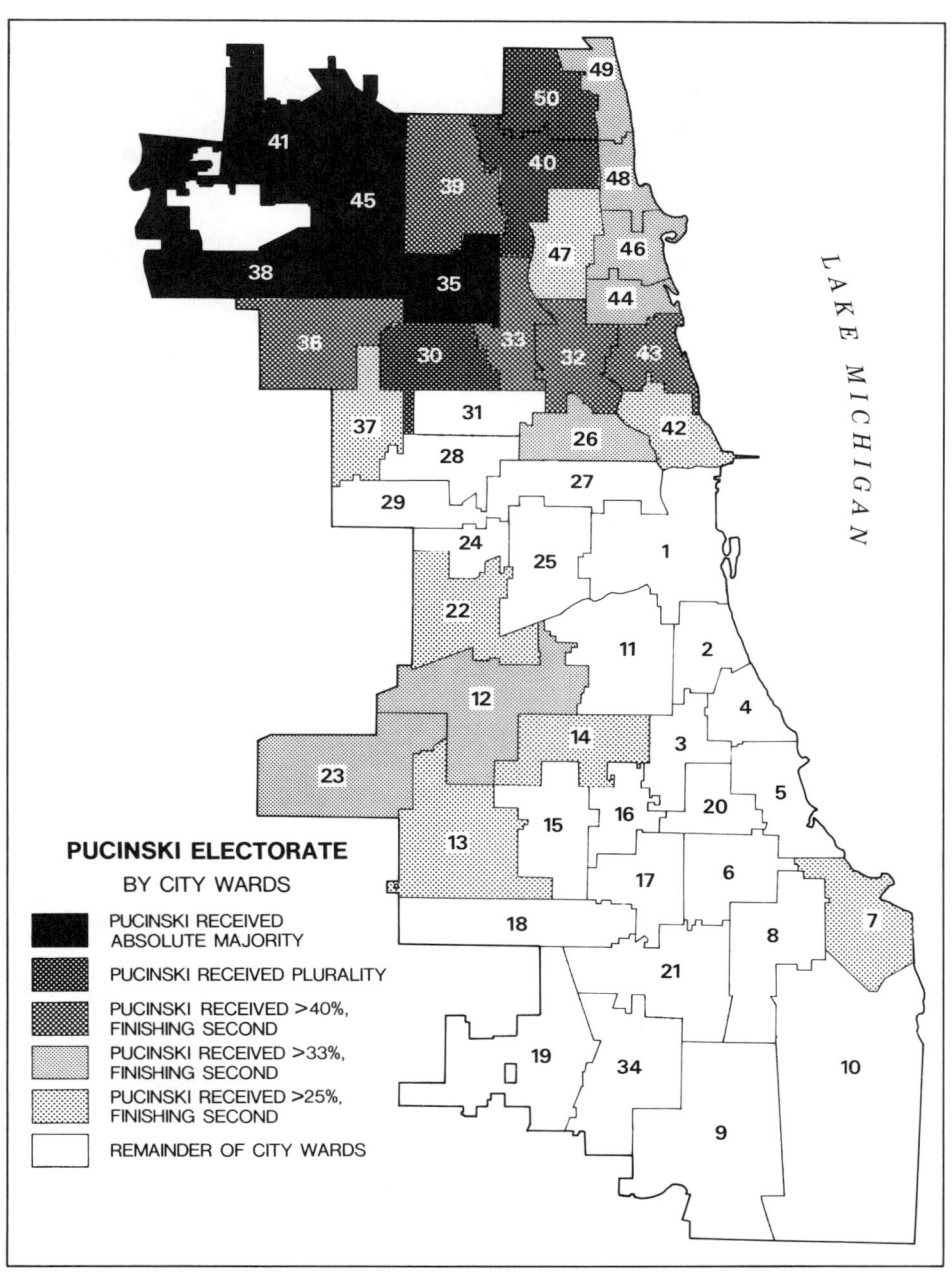

Appendix 2

Selected Characteristics of the Political Systems of Detroit, Buffalo, Milwaukee and Chicago

Characteristics of Municipal Government	Detroit	Buffalo	Milwaukee	Chicago
Form of Government	All Possess the Mayor-Council Form of Government			
Way in Which Mayors are Selected and Their Tenure	Mayor elected in nonpartisan election (4 years)	Mayor elected in partisan election (4 years)	Mayor elected in nonpartisan election (4 years)	Mayor elected in partisan election (4 years)
Way in Which Council is selected (Council size in parentheses)	Nonpartisan, at-large elections (9)	Partisan, aldermanic districts (15), at-large (6)	Nonpartisan, districts (16)	Nonpartisan, districts (50)
Appointive and Patronage Powers of Mayor	Very limited	Significant	Very limited	Very Significant
Nature of Political Competition	Nonpartisan	Democratic Party Dominates	Nonpartisan	Democratic Party Dominates
Dominant Groups in Slating Candidates in Primaries	Unions, Civic Groups important	Erie County Democratic Committee	Union endorsements are important	Cook County Democratic Committee
Highest Elected Municipal Official of Polish Descent	None	Alderman	Alderman	City Clerk
Number of Polish Congressmen	Two (Dingell, Nedzi)	One (Nowak)	One (Zablocki)	Two (Rostenkowski, Fary)
Democratic Vote for President in Each City 1968	71.2%	65.7%	55.4%	60.8%
1972	67.5%	56.4%	55.8%	57.3%
1976	75.4%	62.4%	62.9%	67.4%
Percent of Total Vote of County Cast in City: 1968	53.1%	40.4%	63.8%	61.5%
1972	53.3%	36.1%	62.4%	57.2%
1976	48.9%	32.7%	62.1%	53.1%
Democratic Vote for President: in Surrounding County: 1968	52.3%	48.3%	44.1%	34.3%
1972	37.0%	40.1%	42.0%	30.9%
1976	47.5%	45.3%	46.1%	39.8%

Sources: Richard M. Scammon, ed., *America Votes* (Washington: Government Affairs Institute, Congressional Quarterly, 1969, 1973), volumes 8, 10; *The Municipal Yearbook* (Washington: International City Management Association, 1977).

Appendix 3a.

Ethnic and Racial Characteristics of the Population of Detroit, Federal Censuses of 1900, 1930 and 1970

	City, 1900	City, 1930	City, 1970	Wayne County, 1970
Total Population	285,704	1,440,141	1,511,482	2,666,743
Black Population	4,111	120,066	660,428	721,072
Foreign Born Population	96,503	399,281	119,347	196,884
Foreign Born Plus Children of Foreign Born (1970 Only)	—	—	341,133	635,717
Percent Black	1.4	8.3	43.7	27.0
Percent Foreign Born	33.8	27.7	7.9	7.4
Percent Foreign Born Plus Children of Foreign Born	—	—	22.6	23.8

Leading Immigrant Population Groups in Detroit, 1900 and 1930; Leading Foreign Stock Populations, 1970

City, 1900		City, 1930		City, 1970		County, 1970	
1. Germans	32,027	1. Canadians	81,807	1. Spanish	68,551	1. Canadians	127,196
2. Canadians	28,944	2. Poles	66,113	2. Poles	68,136	2. Poles	115,323
3. Poles	13,631	3. British Isles	56,966	3. Canadians	58,644	3. Spanish	70,732
4. British Isles	8,944	4. Germans	32,716	4. Germans	30,253	4. Italians	56,024
5. Irish	6,412	5. Italians	28,581	5. British	25,474	5. British	55,060

Appendix 3b.

Ethnic and Racial Characteristics of the Population of Buffalo, Federal Censuses of 1900, 1930 and 1970

	City, 1900	City, 1930	City, 1970	Erie County, 1970
Total Population	352,387	558,869	462,781	1,113,491
Black Population	1,698	13,563	94,329	99,238
Foreign Born Population	104,252	118,316	35,252	69,640
Foreign Born Plus Children of Foreign Born (1970 Only)	—	—	130,822	291,635
Percent Black	0.5	2.4	20.4	8.9
Percent Foreign Born	29.6	21.2	7.6	6.1
Percent Foreign Born Plus Children of Foreign Born	—	—	28.3	26.2

Leading Immigrant Population Groups in Buffalo, 1900 and 1930; Leading Foreign Stock Populations, 1970

City, 1900		City, 1930		City, 1970		County, 1970	
1. Germans	36,720	1. Poles	26,616	1. Poles	31,699	1. Poles	65,604
2. Poles	18,830	2. Italians	19,471	2. Italians	29,074	2. Italians	53,698
3. Canadians	17,242	3. Germans	18,816	3. Spanish	16,648	3. Germans	39,339
4. Irish	11,292	4. Canadians	17,884	4. Germans	15,617	4. Canadians	38,354
5. British Isles	8,929	5. British Isles	12,015	5. Canadians	14,008	5. Spanish	25,271

Appendix 3c.

Ethnic and Racial Characteristics of the Population of Milwaukee, Federal Censuses of 1900, 1930 and 1970

	City, 1900	City, 1930	City, 1970	Milwaukee County 1970
Total Population	285,315	568,807	717,372	1,054,249
Black Population	862	7,501	105,088	106,033
Foreign Born Population	88,991	109,383	39,576	54,828
Foreign Born Plus Children of Foreign Born (1970 Only)	—	—	163,492	238,892
Percent Black	0.3	1.3	14.7	10.1
Percent Foreign Born	31.2	19.2	5.5	5.2
Percent Foreign Born Plus Children of Foreign Born	—	—	22.8	22.7

Leading Immigrant Population Groups in Milwaukee, 1900 and 1930; Leading Foreign Stock Populations, 1970

City, 1900		City, 1930		City, 1970		County, 1970	
1. Germans	53,854	1. Germans	40,787	1. Germans	50,237	1. Germans	70,644
2. Poles	17,854	2. Poles	19,593	2. Poles	28,865	2. Poles	39,173
3. Austrians	3,716	3. Russians	7,443	3. Spanish	22,113	3. Spanish	24,949
4. British Isles	3,108	4. Austrians	5,827	4. Italians	8,856	4. Italians	12,607
5. Scandinavians	2,875	5. Yugoslavs	5,647	5. Austrians	7,971	5. Austrians	12,316

Appendix 3d.

Ethnic and Racial Characteristics of the Population of Chicago, Federal Censuses of 1900, 1930 and 1970

	City, 1900	City, 1930	City, 1970	Cook County, 1970
Total Population	1,698,575	3,117,731	3,366,957	5,492,369
Black Population	30,150	233,903	1,102,620	1,183,475
Foreign Born Population	587,112	842,057	373,919	500,742
Foreign Born Plus Children of Foreign Born (1970 Only)	—	—	1,000,982	1,561,082
Percent Black	1.8	7.5	32.7	21.5
Percent Foreign Born	34.6	27.0	11.1	9.1
Percent Foreign Born Plus Children of Foreign Born	—	—	29.7	28.4

Leading Immigrant Population Groups in Chicago, 1900 and 1930; Leading Foreign Stock Populations, 1970

City, 1900		City, 1930		City, 1970		County, 1970	
1. Germans	170,738	1. Poles	149,622	1. Spanish	541,225	1. Spanish	639,617
2. Scandinavians	81,013	2. Germans	111,366	2. Poles	191,955	2. Poles	262,946
3. Irish	73,912	3. Scandinavians	99,977	3. Germans	99,413	3. Germans	173,823
4. Poles	59,713	4. Russians	78,462	4. Italians	97,642	4. Italians	170,120
5. Austrians	53,123	5. Italians	73,970	5. Russians	64,179	5. Russians	95,884

Appendix 4

Polish Americans in Local Elective Offices in Milwaukee

As Ward Aldermen: 1908-1976

Max Kantak, Democrat, 1908-10
Frank Hopp, Democrat, 1908-10+
Martin Gorecki, Socialist, 1910-12+
Anthony Szczerbinski, 1910-12
Leo Krzycki, Socialist, 1912-16
Thomas Szewczykowski, 1912-16
Anton Lukaszewicz, 1916-20
Martin Gedlinski, 1918-20
Casimir Kowalski, Socialist, 1918-22+
John Baranowski, 1918-20
John Suminski, 1918-23*
Albert Janicki, Socialist, 1920-28, 1932-36
Joseph Drzezdzon, 1920-28
Robert Landowski, 1920-28, 1932-36*
Anthony Singer, 1928-32*
Frank Maciolek, Socialist, 1928-32
Max Galasinski, 1928-32
Edward Smukowski, 1928-32
Frank Boncel, Socialist, 1932-36
Felix Lassa, 1932-36
John Kalupa, 1936-48
Clemens Michalski, 1936-52
Bernard Kroenke, 1936-64*
John Schultz, 1936-48
Stanley Cybulski, 1936-48
Jimmy Adamski, 1948-52
Valentine Kujawa, 1948-60
John Gromacki, 1948-56*
Anton Tomczyk, 1952-56
Edmund Choinski, 1952-56
Robert Sulkowski, 1952-56, 1960-72
Richard B. Nowakowski, 1956-68
Ralph Landowski, 1956-60*
John Budzien, 1956-64
Harold Jankowski, 1960-72
Richard Czarnezki, 1968-72
Robert Kordus, 1968-76
Daniel Ziolkowski, since 1976

As State Senators

Michael Kruszka, Democrat, 1892-96
John Kleczka, Republican, 1908-12
Louis Fons, Republican, 1918-20
George Czerwinski, Republican, 1920-24
Walter Polakowski, Socialist, 1922-34
Leonard Fons, Republican, 1930-34
Max Galasinski, Democrat, 1934-38
Arthur Zimny, Democrat, 1934-42
Anthony Gawronski, Democrat, 1938-49
Clement Zablocki, Democrat, 1942-48
Casimir Kendziorski, Democrat, 1949-72
Roman Blenski, Democrat, 1949-54
Richard Zaborski, Democrat, 1954-66*
Ronald Parys, Democrat, 1969-78*
Gerald Kleczka, Democrat, since 1974

As City Comptroller

Roman Czerwinski, Democrat, 1890-94
Peter Pawinski, Democrat, 1902-06
August Gawin, Democrat, 1908-10
Louis Kotecki, 1912-33
John Kalupa, 1958-72

As United States Congressmen

John Kleczka, Republican, 1919-23
Thaddeus Wasielewski, Democrat, 1941-47
Clement Zablocki, Democrat since 1949

As Assemblymen

Francis Borchardt, Democrat, 1882-84
Theodore Rudzinski, Democrat, 1886-88
Michael Kruszka, Democrat, 1890-92
Michael Blenski, Democrat, 1892-94
Andrew Boncel, Democrat, 1894-96
August Gawin, Democrat, 1896-1902
Albert Wojciechowski, Democrat, 1898
Joseph Rechlicz, Democrat, 1898-1900
Frank Hassa, Democrat, 1902-04
John Szymarek, Democrat, 1902-04
Joseph Domachowski, Democrat, 1906-10
Michael Katzban, Socialist, 1910-12
Martin Gorecki, Socialist, 1912-14
Frank Kubatzki, Democrat, 1914-20
Thomas Szewczykowski, Democrat, 1916-18
George Czerwinski, Democrat, 1918-20
John Masiakowski, Socialist, 1918-20
Walter Polakowski, Socialist, 1920-22
Stefan Stolowski, Socialist, 1920-22
John Polakowski, Socialist, 1922-24
Frank Cieszynski, Socialist, 1924-26
Louis Polewczynski, Republican, 1926-28
Alex Chmurski, Republican, 1928-30
Mary Kryszak, Democrat, 1928-30, 1932-38, 1940-44
Joseph Przybylski, Republican, 1928-30
Ben Wicinski, Republican, 1930-32
Martin Franzkowiak, Democrat, 1932-38
Max Galasinski, Democrat, 1932-34
Clemens Michalski, Democrat, 1934-36
Peter Pyszczynski, Democrat, 1936-47
Clement Stachowiak, Progressive, 1938-40
William Nawrocki, Democrat, 1940-44*
Ervin Ryczek, Democrat, 1940-60
Casimir Kendziorski, Democrat, 1946-49
George Sokolowski, Democrat, 1944-60
William Banach, Democrat, 1947-51
Ralph Landowski, Democrat, 1948-56*
Richard B. Nowakowski, Democrat, 1952-56
George Talsky, Democrat, 1954-60
David Mogilka, Democrat, 1956-60
Sherman Sobocinski, Democrat, 1956-62
Raymond Tobiasz, Democrat, 1960-74
Albert Tadych, Democrat, 1960-66
Richard C. Nowakowski, Democrat, 1960-64
Ronald Parys, Democrat, 1964-69*
Robert Kordus, Democrat, 1964-68
Joseph Czerwinski, Democrat, since 1968
Gerald Kleczka, Democrat, 1968-74
John Plewa, Democrat, since 1972
James Rutkowski, Democrat, since 1970
Philip Tuczynski, Democrat, since 1974
Chester Gerlach, Democrat, since 1974

As County Supervisors, 1940-76

Joseph Michalski, 1914-45
Jerome Wroblewski, 1930-60
Leon Szymanski, 1930-60
Henry Wagner, 1945-52
Cornelius Jankowski, 1952-64
Ervin Ryczek, 1960-72
Gerard Skibinski, 1964-72
Richard C. Nowakowski, 1964-74
Emil Stanislawski, since 1972*
Richard Niklewicz, since 1974
Bernadette Skibinski, since 1976
Daniel Kujawa, since 1976

Richard C. Nowakowski served as
  Chairman of the County Board of
  Supervisors, 1972-74

As County Elected Officials

Herman Kubiak, Sheriff, 1948-52,
  Clerk, 1952-60, Democrat
Max Barczak, Sheriff, 1952-56,
  Treasurer, 1956-74, Democrat
Edward Mesheski, Treasurer, 1954-56,
  Democrat
Clemens Michalski, Sheriff, 1956-60,
  Clerk, 1960-68, Democrat
George Witkowski, Sheriff, 1960-62, Democrat
Michael Wolke, Sheriff, 1962-66, and
  since 1968, Democrat
Ronald Witkowiak, Coroner, 1962-66, Democrat
Thomas Zablocki, Clerk, since 1968, Democrat
Walter Barczak, Register of Deeds,
  since 1970, Democrat
Adele Horbinski, Register of Deeds, appointed
  1968-70, Republican

---

*Denotes a North Side Polonia constituency; unless otherwise noted, candidates were elected as nonpartisans
+elected as an alderman at-large

Published by Haertlein Graphics, Milwaukee, Wisconsin

PT349 '425